THE COAL STRIKE

NEW CITY PAPERBACKS

Edited by John J. Vincent

New City Paperbacks are designed to tell some of the stories of urban life in Britain.

The urban scene has attracted many commentators, sociologists, analysts, problem-solvers and planners. We have seen the tragic effects of some of their ideas. But this series has a different intention. Our intention is to try to start rebuilding the city "from the bottom". But how can we do it? I know of only one way – to begin to gather together the remnants of humanity and value that are still there – the histories, the stories, the characters, the communities, the songs, the poems, the people, the traditions.

So, we publish **New City Paperbacks** not as a collection of antiques or curiosities, but as a prophecy for the future, as a call to discover what we want, what we can build on, and what models and paradigms we might use for the future.

THE COAL STRIKE

Christian Reflections on the Miners' Struggle

Brian Jenner

NEW CITY

ISBN 0 907490 01 8

First published 1986 by

NEW CITY
Urban Theology Unit
210 Abbeyfield Road,
Sheffield, S4 7AZ

Printed in Great Britain by
A. Wheaton & Co. Ltd.,
Hennock Road, Marsh Barton, Exeter,
EX2 8RP

CONTENTS

PREFACE

The coal strike of 1984-5 was one of the most significant industrial and political episodes in modern British history. In the following pages, we tell something of the story of the strike, and we offer reflections upon it. The book has been written by a group of people, all of whom happened to be living in Barnsley, at the heart of the Yorkshire coal field, at the time the strike took place.

That being so, we could not but be affected by the events happening around us. We believe that our particular view of those events has given us a story worth telling.

We have not tried to write a definitive account of the strike, nor to deal systematically with all the issues it raised. Our support for the fundamental aims of the miners in their resistance to pit closures and their struggle to maintain the life of their communities is, we hope, apparent in what we have written. That, of course, does not mean that we necessarily support every action taken by every striker, nor every decision of the miners' leaders. At the same time, we have not thought it necessary to raise all the critical questions which might be raised about some aspects of the strike.

This is also, quite specifically, a book of *Christian* story-telling and reflection. We have sought throughout to bring our Christian commitment to bear upon the events we describe. Through our own process of reflection upon the struggles of people around us and upon our own commitment to supporting those struggles, we have re-discovered something of the significance of Christian discipleship in Britain today. Our conviction has grown that the events we have witnessed have a significance far greater than many have perceived.

The strike was undoubtedly a time of struggle. It was also a time when new solidarity was discovered. Christians, as well as people of other faiths and of none, played their part in supporting those who were struggling for justice for themselves and for their communities. One small sign of that solidarity was the 'Christian Support for Mining Communities' fund, which raised over £9,000 from Christians in this country and abroad. We say thank you to all who gave practical support at a time when it was greatly needed.

We dedicate this book to the people of Barnsley, and to all others 'who hunger and thirst to see right prevail' (Matt 5:6).

May the struggle not be in vain.

BRIAN JENNER: January 1986

MEMBERS OF THE GROUP

The following people shared in writing this book.

JANE GROUT:
Methodist Local Preacher; Estate Agent in a mining village near Barnsley.

BRIAN JENNER:
Methodist Minister; member until August 1985 of the Barnsley Team Ministry, and now working in Co. Durham.

MICK LAND:
Teacher at Thurnscoe Comprehensive School; a native of Barnsley.

GEOFF REID:
Methodist Minister; member of the Barnsley Team Ministry; Liberal Candidate for Barnsley Central in the 1983 General Election.

EILEEN SANDERSON:
Member of Hoyland Methodist Church; Local Preacher On Trial; employed by Barnsley Metropolitan Borough Council as a Play Leader.

GLYNIS SHARPE:
Regional Development Officer, Trent and Yorkshire MIND (National Association for Mental Health); Treasurer to the Team Council of the Barnsley Team Ministry.

MICHAEL WEDGEWORTH:
Methodist Minister; Head of the Employment Division, Barnsley Metropolitan Borough Council; Secretary of the Coalfields Communities Campaign.

There was one other member of the group whose name, for professional reasons, cannot be publicly quoted.

In addition, Chapter Nine draws extensively upon material presented by MICHAEL WEST (Senior Chaplain, Sheffield Industrial Mission), at a conference organised by the Barnsley Team Ministry in June 1985 to consider questions of ministry and mission in the aftermath of the strike. We are grateful to Mike for his co-operation in making this material available.

A NOTE ON ABBREVIATIONS

We use a number of abbreviated titles in the following pages. Most of our readers, we think, will have no great difficulty with them, but the following list may help prevent occasional bafflement.

ACPO	Association of Chief Police Officers
CEGB	Central Electricity Generating Board
DHSS	Department of Health and Social Security
NACODS	National Association of Colliery Overmen, Deputies and Shotfirers
NCB	National Coal Board
NCCL	National Council for Civil Liberties
NRC	National Reporting Centre
NUM	National Union of Mineworkers
TUC	Trades Union Congress

ACKNOWLEDGMENTS

We are grateful to John Vincent, at the Urban Theology Unit, for his encouragement and help in making possible the publication of this book, and to Margaret Mackley and Grace Vincent, who read the typescript and made many valuable suggestions for improvements in presentation.

CHAPTER ONE

COAL OR DOLE?

The village of Thurnscoe lies about seven miles east of the centre of Barnsley, overlooking the valley of the River Dearne, in the heart of the Yorkshire coalfield. The population of the village, some 11,445, would make it almost a small town, but in many ways Thurnscoe remains a village. The life of the community is insular in many ways. Mobility of the population is low—eighty per cent of employed people there travel less than three miles to work. Social life centres upon the immediate neighbourhood with its local groupings – families, brass bands, union lodges, church congregations, pub clienteles and club memberships.

The life of the community exhibits features common to most close working class communities: a lack of privacy and rapid transfer of information, a lack of individual competitiveness, pervasive conformity to role and status expectations, a lack of self-confidence (usually masked in males by an outwardly macho image). Levels of aspiration are low, and traditional expectations encouraged. The village is almost entirely dependent upon the mining industry.

Thurnscoe grew up in the 19th century around the pits owned by Lord Halifax. The village pit, Hickleton Colliery, is a descendant from those origins, and still today the National Coal Board (NCB) remains the major source of male employment, providing no less than sixty-four per cent of all male employment in the village according to the 1981 census. Indeed, within South Yorkshire, the Dearne Thurnscoe Ward has the highest proportion of resident males working in coal mining – closely followed by the neighbouring Ward of Brierley (which includes Goldthorpe). Yet, even so, coal mining as a source of employment has in recent years been in decline. From 1,251 in 1977, the workforce at Hickleton Colliery had fallen by 1983 to 685.

Outside mining, opportunities are few. Full-time jobs for women form only twelve per cent of the local total, while only six per cent of local jobs are classified in the 1981 census as 'Professional and Managerial' – contrasting with the national average of about one third. As in the rest of the Dearne Valley, unemployment is high, and the threat of even greater levels of unemployment when the pit closes now hangs over the village. Indeed, even before the MacGregor proposals for re-organisation of the mining industry, the future of Hickleton Colliery was in doubt. At the time of the 1981 census, unemployment among the 'economically active' – broadly, those capable of work – was twenty per cent. Without the NCB, that figure would rise to over seventy per cent. Meanwhile, in 1981 even twenty per cent was twice the national average.

Employment prospects for the young are even more depressing. Even before the proposed NCB reorganisation the prospects for young males could hardly have been worse. Adults, at least, are cushioned to some extent by redundancy payments, but for the young the disappearance of mining leaves virtually no opportunities of any kind. In 1977, out of 185 school leavers in Thurnscoe, only 20 were either unemployed or on a government scheme. By 1984, out of 215 school leavers, 126 were unemployed or on a scheme. The number going on to further education had increased, but that would include a good many who did so only reluctantly, and who later would drop out to re-appear in the unemployment statistics.

Again, in 1977 the NCB took 61 leavers from Thurnscoe Comprehensive School into apprenticeships. In 1983 only 3 were taken, and none at all in 1984. Indeed, Barnsley College of Technology no longer provides mining training courses, and nowhere in the UK does the NCB now sponsor any electrical or mechanical engineering apprenticeships. Yet as recently as 1981, Barnsley College of Technology had 150 mining apprentices. In villages like Thurnscoe, the withdrawal of NCB opportunities has almost totally destroyed local employment prospects for young males, while the prospects for girls are hardly brighter.

With unemployment comes poverty, which in Thurnscoe is undoubtedly increasing. Not only the unemployed, but also the old, single-parent families, the sick, the disabled, and those on low pay share the afflictions of poverty. The depressing and depressed faces at the local post office on 'Giro day' are a testament to the impact of poverty and unemployment on the life of the community. Poverty and unemployment lead to demoralisation and impotence. Failure and the fear of failure sets up psychological barriers, while tending to exhibit itself as an attitude of 'I don't care anyway'. The outcome may be drunkenness, fighting, criminality, wife- and child-beating, or proving one's virility and fertility by having unplanned children. Increasingly, a sense of despair comes to pervade the whole community.

Against such a background, it is not difficult to understand the solidarity of the miners in places like Thurnscoe throughout the twelve months of the coal strike. As always, the simple media images were gross distortions of a far-from-simple reality.

Fear was certainly part of the story, although fear of intimidation was by no means the whole, nor the most important truth. There was fear of intimidation, certainly, and fear, too, of what might happen to strikebreakers once it was all over. Two or three minutes in a descending pit cage can be a long time when there are old scores to be settled. As if to underline the point, there are stories of more than one strikebreaker who since the end of the strike has moved with his family from Yorkshire to more hospitable places like Nottinghamshire.

But there was another, more important fear: the fear of unemployment. Thurnscoe was by no means the only place in South Yorkshire where, even before the strike, the unemployment rate was well over 20%. Many such communities remain entirely dependent upon mining for their very existence. There was fear, therefore, of new technologies. There was fear of new coalfields like Selby. There was fear that what happened in County Durham in the 1950s and 1960s, when whole villages were destroyed – socially and sometimes physically – might happen in South Yorkshire, too. Since the end of the strike, nothing has happened to suggest that those fears were misplaced. Rather, much has happened to confirm them.

There was fear, and there was anger. Again contrary to some of the media images, support for the NUM leadership, personified in Arthur Scargill, was by no means total and by no means uncritical, even in 'militant' South Yorkshire. But if hard things were sometimes said against their own leaders, it was for Margaret Thatcher and Ian MacGregor that the real anger was reserved. Few of the Yorkshire miners seriously doubted that the Tories deliberately chose conflict with the NUM. Two years previously it had been avoided, but now the loyalty of police and judiciary was assured after massive pay rises. The appointment of MacGregor to run the NCB was seen as a clear declaration of war and, indeed, the confrontational style in which he handled the dispute, and which has hardly abated since its end, brought dismay to many senior Coal Board officials. Like pay restraint in the public sector, like cuts and privatisation in health, education and the social services, like the banning of trade unions at GCHQ, the attempt to destroy the NUM was seen as another step in an all-out attack on the British working class.

Fear and anger – but there was reason, too. The strike was by no means simply a powerful emotional outburst. People in the mining industry are well aware that, however much re-structuring of the industry may be necessary, nevertheless a simple distinction between 'economic' and 'uneconomic' pits cannot be sustained, and, behind the NUM's case if too rarely expressed, there was some sophisticated economic analysis.

We shall have more to say about this in Chapter Eight. For the moment, we simply note that the term 'uneconomic pit' represents little more than an arbitrary judgment based on short-term financial considerations. It says nothing about the long-term prospects of a pit; nothing about the social and economic costs of unemployment; nothing about the long-term consequences, economic and political, of greater dependence upon imported oil and uranium. When such considerations are taken into account, it is not difficult to support the NUM's view that it can often cost more to close pits than to keep them open.

To fear, anger and reason was added mistrust. There was wide recognition of the way in which under Margaret Thatcher the nation has become increasingly divided: there is a wealthy and privileged nation, and there is an oppressed and depressed one. There was recognition that, however well-paid some miners may have been, the pay has been little recompense not only for the physical unpleasantness of the work, but also for the massive deprivation which still exists – by whatever indices you may choose to measure it. There was recognition that, whosever side she may have been on, Margaret Thatcher certainly was not, and is not, on 'our' side, and a deep unwillingness to trust promises of pay or re-deployment made by her or her agents. 'After all, they promised us five years' work at Cortonwood, then they threatened to shut it within a year'.

In Barnsley, as elsewhere in the country, as the strike progressed you could hear opinions of all sorts about it. Here, however, the contradictory opinions were often expressed by the same person. The tensions were not only, nor primarily, between different groups; they were inside everyone. People were torn apart emotionally. Marriages were destroyed. Yet there was, too, a real solidarity – a solidarity which had grown through years of struggle, and which was re-discovered and strengthened as more and more people needed to rely on others for even the most basic necessities of life ('I can't wait for Christmas', said one miner's wife in September. 'We're going to light a fire then!').

The miners' strike was about the future of the coal industry. It was about the future of men, women and children, and of whole communities threatened by pit closures. It was about a Tory Government's intention to destroy the power of working people.

In the following pages, we tell something of the story of the coal strike of 1984-5. We are not the only people to tell the story – others have already done so, and more no doubt will do so. We tell it, however, in our particular way, from our own perspective – as Christians who lived in Barnsley at the time, and who, like everyone else, could not but be caught up, in one way and another, in events which were happening all around us. We tell it as we saw it, recognising that others saw it differently. We tell it, recognising that our response, like that of most of our fellow-Christians, was quite inadequate. What we did was not enough, and we did it too late.

We tell the story, and we offer our reflections upon it, not only because the experience of living through the strike was such a powerful experience, but also because of the faith we hold. With our fellow-Christians throughout the ages, we believe that the Jesus whom we worship is Lord of all the world, and that God's Holy Spirit is constantly at work, seeking to bring liberation for all people from all that holds us in bondage and prevents us from being fully the people whom God created us to be. If Jesus is Lord, we believe, then he is Lord over the world's political and economic structures. If the Spirit brings liberation, then she is the creator of freedom from economic want and political oppression. And if that is so, then as Christians we cannot ignore the struggles of the men and women among whom we live. In every human struggle for greater justice, in every struggle of the weak for more power over the things that affect their own lives, God's Spirit is also at work.

In reflecting upon our story, we have learned important things about the resources that faith has to offer. We believe that those lessons are lessons to be shared, and we trust that, in sharing them, we may have something to say not only to other Christians in Britain's mining communities but to others, too, both within the mining communities and beyond. God's word comes to us out of the turmoil of the world in which he has placed us. We hope that by sharing our attempt to hear that word, we may encourage others to make their attempts, too – not only to hear the word, but also to do it.

CHAPTER TWO

THE STORY

The strike is over after twelve months of strife. A Yorkshire miner, standing in a steady drizzle outside TUC headquarters in London's Great Russell Street, is losing his own personal battle to hold back his tears.

He struggles to find words that will most adequately reflect the deep desolation, frustration and anger he feels. After the hardest year of his life, so much sacrifice seems to have brought so little reward.

Inside TUC headquarters, National Union of Mineworkers (NUM) delegates have decided, by 98 votes to 91, on a return to work without any agreement with the NCB on the issues that prompted the dispute. When the miner does find words, they simply state fact. 'We've given our hearts, we've given our blood, we've given our souls', he says, and walks away weeping.

For others throughout the British coalfields, the reaction is not one of bitterness. Many miners feel great relief that a dispute which has put them through a physical and mental mangle, gouged holes in the fabric of their closely-knit communities and, in some cases, left them thousands of pounds in debt, has at last run its course.

The strike began officially on March 8th 1984, when the NUM's National Executive, meeting at its Sheffield headquarters, officially sanctioned plans by Yorkshire and Scottish miners to strike from the following Monday, March 12th, and said that similar action in other coalfields would also be official. There would, however, be no national ballot of the union's 180,000 members. The Yorkshire NUM's anger had been apparent since March 1st, when the Coal Board had nominated two South Yorkshire collieries near Barnsley – Cortonwood and Bullcliffe Wood – for closure on economic grounds.

Immediately, 9,000 men walk out, and the strike is soon spreading to other parts of Yorkshire. The Scottish NUM also calls for a strike over the closure of Scottish pits. Meanwhile, the Coal Board announces plans to cut four million tonnes of capacity, and spells out the terms for any mine workers volunteering to leave the industry: a golden handshake of £1,000 for each year of service to miners under 49 with more than five years of service. Redundancy payments for miners over 49 would remain unaltered. 'The aim', says a Board spokesman, 'is a reduction in manpower, with cash acting as a palliative'.

The Board also issues figures showing that Britain's mine workers were earning an average of £167.47 per week, including overtime, before stoppages. National average earnings for male manual workers at the time were £153.60. Among the miners, the highest paid were the 22,000 underground craftsmen, fitters and electricians, whose gross wage averaged £198.60 per week. Of that, £32.24 was overtime.

The NUM Executive's decision to sanction strike action brings a warning from the Department of Employment that any attempts by 'flying pickets' – from Yorkshire or Scotland – to encourage more widespread action in other parts of the country will be deemed unlawful, as all forms of secondary action are banned under the 1980 Employment Act. Meanwhile Mr Arthur Scargill, President of the NUM, says he has no idea how the dispute will develop, but that the Coal Board and its Chairman Mr Ian MacGregor will have to take responsibility for whatever takes place.

On March 12th, the first official day of the strike all 53 pits in the Yorkshire coalfield are at a standstill. Soon, however, there are signs that Yorkshire's unity is not to be found in all areas. In the country as a whole, only about a half of the miners are on strike. In Nottinghamshire there is particularly strong opposition to the strike, and 'rebel' pits still working are subjected to increasingly heavy picketing. In an attempt to stop it, the Board asks for, and is granted, a High Court injunction ordering the Yorkshire NUM to confine pickets to pits in their own area.

Next day, however – March 15th – Yorkshire pickets are again out in force in Nottinghamshire, and their leaders say they will continue to follow normal, established trade union practices to win solidarity and to save pits and jobs. Police from Essex and Cumbria join others drafted into Nottinghamshire, and Mr Scargill appeals to his members to 'behave responsibly'. He adds that he wants to see the union in total unity against the NCB, to keep pits open and jobs secure. The real enemies, to whom attention should be directed, are the NCB and the Government.

March 15th also sees the first death on a picket line, at Ollerton Colliery, Notts. A Home Office pathologist says that 24-year-old Yorkshire miner David Jones, a father of two children from South Kirby, Barnsley, could have come into forcible contact with a solid object such as a post, a wheel or a vehicle. He rules out a fatal blow from a brick or a truncheon, and says there is no indication that Mr Jones had been assaulted by anyone.

Going to the scene, Mr Scargill calls for two minutes' silence for Mr Jones. In a moving gesture, policemen take off their helmets and stand alongside the pickets. Mr Scargill tells the pickets, 'Let's hope this miner did not die in vain', and Mr MacGregor describes Mr Jones' death as a 'tragic incident'.

March 16th, in a significant development, sees the Midlands, Lancashire and South Derbyshire areas all vote against striking. Yorkshire's pickets immediately move into the Midlands, joining miners from South Wales and Kent. They manage to close nine pits out of eleven. The NCB apply for an order to start contempt of court proceedings against the NUM, on the grounds that by sending pickets into other areas they have flouted a court order. Mr Justice Nolan takes ten minutes to approve the NCB's application, but three days later the Board decide against a High Court battle and drop the proceedings.

Towards the end of March, the Central Electricity Generating Board claims that power station coal stocks are at a record level for the time of year, while Mr MacGregor says he will hold out 'indefinitely' against strikers who, by now, have left only 37 of Britain's 176 pits working normally. By the middle of March only one miner in Yorkshire is left working, Bob Coppins, a winder from Little Houghton. He gives up his solo protest when threats upset him and his car is turned over outside his home. In Barnsley, there is concern about the role police are playing on picket lines: some Labour members of Barnsley District Council suggest that overtime pay to South Yorkshire police should be stopped, and restored only if they are withdrawn from picket line duty.

Also toward the end of March, wives of Barnsley miners decide to join the picket lines outside the NCB's Barnsley Area headquarters at

Grimethorpe. More than thirty women from the Barnsley Women Against Pit Closures group join the picket. At about the same time, food kitchens open in Barnsley for the first time in fifty years: the District Council offers use of the Civic Hall and supervisory staff free of charge to the NUM, to organise hot food for the miners and their families.

In mid-April, Barnsley East MP Mr Terry Patchett claims that police have been bugging miners' telephones. False information, he says, deliberately put out by miners in telephone conversations, had resulted in police arriving at a hoax meeting place. South Yorkshire's Acting Chief Constable denies the claim.

Help for the miners comes from many quarters. Entertainers offer their services free in the local clubs. Tommy Hampshire, a former Yorkshire club singer, comes out of retirement at the age of 82 to sing in a money-raising concert, and a 79-year-old disabled man from Mexborough hands over his savings of £1,000 because he does not want children to suffer as they did in 1926.

On April 20th, a special NUM Delegate Conference votes down four resolutions calling for a national ballot. It also votes, by 187,000 to 59,000, to change the union rules so that in future a simple majority, rather than 55 per cent, will be sufficient for calling a national strike.

As summer approaches, picketing intensifies. More than 100 pickets are arrested at Creswell Colliery in Derbyshire. On May 16th, Mr Scargill's wife Anne is arrested on a Nottinghamshire picket line, and two weeks later Mr Scargill himself is arrested for alleged obstruction on a picket line at Orgreave Coking Plant, South Yorkshire. On May 25th, a High Court judge declares the strike to be unconstitutional, and grants injunctions to 631 Nottinghamshire miners, banning the union from instructing them to stop work.

A month later comes possibly the blackest day yet. As the situation erupts at Orgreave, 80 are injured including Mr Scargill and 28 policemen, and 100 are arrested.

By July, several rounds of peace talks between the NUM and the NCB have collapsed. The chief sticking point is the definition of what constitutes an 'exhausted' pit.

Also early in July, a Barnsley Methodist minister states in public that miners are not violent people. The Revd Denis Gardiner tells the Methodist Conference, meeting in Wolverhampton, that 'Barnsley is not a violent part of the country, and the men I know are not the pawns of demagogic leaders or politicians. They fear not only for their jobs but also for their communities'.

July, however, sees mobs running wild in the pit villages of Hemsworth, Kinsley and Fitzwilliam, all near Barnsley. The police station at Hemsworth is attacked, vehicles are set on fire, and NCB offices damaged. Trains are stopped on the main London railway line because, police say, 'it was not safe for them to go through'. On subsequent weekends there is similar trouble at Wombwell and Grimethorpe.

A national dock strike is called in July. The British Steel Corporation have shipped coal to Scunthorpe via Immingham docks, and the unions involved attempt to stop ferry traffic through Dover in retaliation. Because of the hostile reaction from stranded lorry drivers, however, the Dover dockers call off the stoppage and after thirteen days the dock strike collapses.

The end of the month sees the full force of the law used against the South Wales NUM, when they are fined £50,000 for contempt of court after defying an order to stop picketing the Port Talbot steelworks. They refuse to pay the fine, and a sequestrator is appointed by the court.

In Nottinghamshire, a back-to-work movement emerges, led by an anonymous miner known, because of the colour of his hair, as 'Silver Birch'. He visits several coalfields in the hope of persuading striking miners to go back to work, and he is eventually identified as Mr Chris Butcher, a blacksmith at Bevercotes Colliery, Notts. His home is in Ollerton, the scene of some of the most violent clashes between pickets and police.

The first small sign of a crack in Yorkshire's solidarity appears in the middle of August, when the first Yorkshire miner returns to work at Gascoigne Wood Colliery, Selby. He runs the gauntlet of four hundred pickets, and the Coal Board say they do not see his lone action as evidence of a general drift back to work. They do view as significant, however, the return to work a week later of seventeen miners at various Yorkshire pits.

In September, the TUC weighs in with support for the miners, but the steel and electricians' unions are reluctant to commit themselves to positive action. There is a surprising turn in the dispute however, when NACODS, the pit deputies' union, votes in favour of a strike because the Coal Board intends to stop paying NACODS members who will not cross picket lines. The union agrees to talk to the Board, and eventually calls off its strike after being offered concessions.

On October 3rd, Barnsley experiences violence when police and pickets fight at Woolley Colliery after a lone miner goes through a picket line with a police escort. Three policemen are taken to hospital. A week later, the miner is attacked at 6.30 in the morning while on his way to meet a van which was to take him to work. He is discharged after treatment at Barnsley District General Hospital for facial injuries.

The Coal Board warn that at least twelve coal faces in the Barnsley area are causing concern, and declare that the situation will deteriorate unless the strike ends soon.

Also in early October the NUM is fined £200,000 and Mr Scargill £1,000 for contempt of court. It is the start of a series of legal actions which lead to the High Court's appointing sequestrators to sieze the NUM's assets after the union refuses to pay the fine. An unknown donor pays Mr Scargill's fine.

Signs of tensions within the top level management of the NCB appear when Mr Michael Eaton is suddenly appointed as spokesman for the Board, and then almost immediately removed. Meanwhile Mr Geoffrey Kirk, chief of the PR section, is first reported to be 'on holiday', but then leaves his job.

At the start of November, the Board offers any miner returning to work £650 in pre-Christmas pay packets. By November 5th about nine hundred have accepted the offer and the Secretary of State for Energy, Mr Peter Walker, declares that the strike is crumbling. By November 13th five thousand have returned. In the Barnsley Area, however, only eight men are at work.

On November 3rd, NUM assets totalling £2.7 million are frozen in a Dublin bank at the request of the sequestrators. £4 million is traced to Luxembourg and £500,000 to Zurich. On November 30th a Receiver is appointed to control the union's assets.

On November 20th the North Wales NUM withdraws its support for the strike. Leaders say that the men have voted with their feet for a return. By the end of the month, the NCB is claiming that 68,000 miners are working at 146 pits. Meanwhile, the legal fight continues over control of union assets.

November 30th sees the most horrific incident since the start of the strike when a taxi driver taking a miner to work in South Wales is killed by a three-feet-long concrete post thrown on to his vehicle from an overhead bridge. Two miners are later charged with murder.

As Christmas approaches, TUC General Secretary Mr Norman Willis leads a 'peace mission' to meet with Mr Peter Walker, the Energy Secretary, but it leads nowhere.

In the period leading up to Christmas, help and support comes from many quarters. A week before Christmas, Barnsley Team Ministry receive 4 tonnes of toys donated by German steel workers. A church hall is used as a distribution centre and within a couple of days the NUM have arranged distribution of all the toys.

The Coal Board write to miners during the Christmas period spelling out details of tax-free money which could be earned before the end of the financial year. In the first two weeks of January 1985, 4,400 more men return to work, and pressure mounts upon the NUM leadership. By the end of the month the drift back has turned into a flood. On February 4th, 2,318 go back to work – a record for one day.

Hopes for a peaceful settlement rise to their highest level for months when the NUM's Executive meets on February 15th to hear a report from Norman Willis, TUC General Secretary, on his meetings with Mr MacGregor; but hopes crash when the Board announces it is not prepared to accept the latest proposals. Mr Willis says the gap between the parties is so small that, in industrial relations terms, it is bridgeable.

Following a meeting at Downing Street, Mrs Thatcher re-iterates that any resolution of the dispute must deal clearly and unambiguously with its central issue, that of the Board's right to close uneconomic pits.

NUM delegates meet for a special conference in London on February 21st and unanimously back the Executive's continuing stand, but the following day there are reports of large numbers of miners returning to work. In Yorkshire, a total of 7,650 are now at work. By February 26th, the Board are claiming that 91,000 – a half of all Britain's miners – are now at work.

On March 3rd it is all over. NUM delegates vote to return to work without an agreement.

CHAPTER THREE

THE CHURCHES

'The people of Cortonwood chapel gave and gave 'til they had no more, then they gave again'. That is how one person described the response of one Methodist chapel to the plight of the community in which its members lived.

Cortonwood was the place where the strike began. Everyone knows that. Cortonwood's chapel is less well known. It is a large building. Its membership is small and elderly, and, when the strike was at its height, the chapel was stricken by a seemingly overwhelming problem. Wet rot and dry rot were discovered in the building, and the cost of the necessary repairs was estimated at £5,000.

The response of the people of Cortonwood – not just the people of the chapel, but many others too – was staggering. Within a month the church, with only 29 members, raised nearly £4,000. 'The local folk, so weighed down with their own troubles, went out of their way to show us that they cared and told us: "We love our little chapel!"'. A tiny, struggling congregation, which nevertheless had not failed to give what support it could to those around it, was receiving support in return.

Cortonwood was not the only small congregation in Barnsley to offer support for those struggling for the survival of their communities. Elsewhere, weekly collections were taken to support the miners. Support of other kinds was given. In general, it seems that it was the churches which themselves felt their survival to be most under threat which responded most readily to the miners around them.

It is hard to say how far people directly involved in the dispute expected support from the churches. Most of them are people who have little connection with the church, and probably the majority of striking miners and their families hardly gave the church a second thought. A survey which was conducted within the Barnsley Methodist Circuit towards the end of the strike showed just how tenuous the church's links with the miners have become. In Barnsley as elsewhere, the great bulk of church members are elderly, while of those who are in employment, only 1 in 5 were working miners – no more than two per cent of the overall membership. Only half the churches which responded reported that they had miners as members; perhaps more surprisingly, only a similar proportion reported links with mining families through their 'Community Roll'. Not surprisingly, it was to the miners' welfare institutes, the Labour Party, parents, relatives, friends, and fellow strikers that those needing help turned, and from those sources that most of the necessary support was received.

Within the churches, there were a few who hoped for a vigorous response to people's needs as the dispute unfolded. Reminders were given of the strong historical links of the Methodist and other, mostly non-conformist, churches with the early trade union movement. Appeal was made to the precedents of Christian involvement in the fight for the abolition of slavery, of Christian concern for improving working conditions in the early years of this century, of Christian pressure today to relieve the suffering of millions in the world because of hunger, injustice and oppression.

Yet when the church responded officially, whether nationally through figures like the Bishop of Durham, the Archbishop of Canterbury or the President of the Methodist Conference, or more locally through well-informed clergy and lay people, by no means everyone welcomed such 'interference'. Some resented it. One response to the news that a senior clergyman was to address a union meeting was along the lines of 'What has the church to do with it? He's never been down a pit!' Others welcomed the involvement as an indication that the church was willing to play some part, but many, including large numbers of church members, shouted long and hard that the church should stick to things spiritual. Many more, meanwhile, probably remained both unaware and unconcerned, or kept silent because they felt it was 'nothing to do with them'.

Nevertheless, there were some Christians who believed that it was vital that the church should make some response, that it should play some role in the face of the hardship and strife which afflicted the people whose lives it was called to serve. Thus, in the summer of 1984, a fund was established by the Superintendent Minister of the Barnsley Methodist Circuit. A letter was sent to all the Methodist churches in the area, asking for contributions to be distributed through the NUM's own Solidarity Fund. A number of churches took special collections, and some donated from their church funds. In some places, however, there was anger at the suggestion that support should be given through the NUM. 'How can we know', it was asked, 'that the money will go to people who really need it?'

The number of churches which directly supported the fund was quite small, although it seems likely that the discussion to which the Superintendent's letter gave rise did have some good side-effects. The issue was raised, and some churches which were not prepared to support the fund did nevertheless begin to look beyond the limits of their own walls and to ask if there were not things they should be doing. Some churches organised food parcels for families in the area. Miners who had connections with the church in most cases seem to have received both financial and other support from the churches, or from friends within the church. Other individuals within the churches gave generous support to people whose need they personally knew about. There were those who responded positively to the injunction of Jesus to love not only those who love us (Mt 5:46); but it has to be added that there were few of whom it could be said that there was 'no limit to their goodness' (Mt 5:48). In general, much of the response was that of Christian individuals rather than of the church as a body, and much of it was the generous response of one friend or neighbour to another – of a kind which was given also by many who had no connection with the church.

The organised response of the church was small in scale and patchy in extent; and it was entirely at the level of supporting individuals in immediate need. Nowhere was there any response to the larger issues raised by the strike itself. Nowhere was there any indication that the churches were prepared to express support for the aims of the miners, or commit themselves to sharing in the struggle for the very life of the communities in which they were set. The reasons why this should have been so we shall have to consider shortly.

Towards the end of 1984, with the approach of Christmas, there was a noticeable improvement in response to the needs of families, and particularly of children. Most church members seem to have felt that children should not have to suffer because of the dispute in which their fathers were involved. When a lorry-load of toys arrived from Germany, just a few days before Christmas, there was no difficulty in finding a church hall to be used as a distribution-centre, nor in finding church members willing to help with the unloading. Some church buildings were used for children's parties, while other churches held collections to help finance parties held elsewhere, including some organised by the miners and their support groups. Financial help was also given to try to ensure that every child had at least one present, and more if possible, to open on Christmas Day.

Christmas, and the feelings aroused by the thought of people spending the season in misery, encouraged the greatest involvement of the churches. Afterwards, however, the pattern very quickly returned to the earlier detached silence, and even at Christmas there was much anxiety to maintain the distinction between caring for people in need and appearing to support a cause with which many had little if any sympathy. To give financial assistance was acceptable, but many Christian miners seem to have felt a lack of moral and spiritual support from their fellow Christians, particularly if they broadly supported the objectives of the strike. Those Christian miners who were known to feel that they should not be on strike, and who continued to withhold their labour only because of fear or of loyalty to the union, seem to have received more of the support they needed to cope with the mental strains to which they were subject.

There was, then, a general feeling within the churches of being 'anti-strike', and this judgment was borne out by the results of the survey within the Barnsley Circuit. Why should it have been so?

One reason seems to be that there was generally an inability to separate the feelings aroused by media coverage of the strike, and particularly of the more violent aspects of its conduct, from the objectives toward which the strike was directed. Horror at the violence, and a conviction that the union leadership had made many mistakes, over-rode any perception of the purpose of it all and of the reasons why people were finding themselves compelled to take such action.

Another reason seems to have been a very great fear that the divisions the strike seemed to be opening in the community at large might very easily disrupt the life of the churches as well. There was a deep reluctance within the church to discuss the issues involved. When, even after the strike was over, the Barnsley Methodist Circuit Meeting eventually did discuss the strike and its consequences, a resolution which came no nearer to supporting the miners than to express the conviction that 'any decision on pit closures must take account both of economic and of social factors' was passed by 18 votes to none – but with some 30 or more abstentions, so difficult was it for people to express their convictions. Similarly, when the survey into responses to the strike was carried out in the Circuit, not all churches returned the questionnaire. Some, it seems, feared that merely to complete a very simple questionnaire would open wounds and expose hurts which were better left hidden.

Then, there were theological reasons. As a formal and academic discipline, theology has little place in the life of the churches in Barnsley. There is, nevertheless, an important folk theology, whose effects are deeply pervasive. If there is one word which sums up that theology, the word is 'pietism'. In the Anglican churches, the catholic tradition is strongly represented (much of Barnsley, after all, is in the strongly 'high church' Diocese of Wakefield); the Free Churches tend to be basically evangelical, and there are considerable congregationalist tendencies, encouraged in Methodists by a significant Wesleyan Reform presence. In all denominations, however, there is an overriding individualism and other-worldliness. The churches exist to comfort individuals in this life, and to prepare them for the next. If there is any social ethic at all implied by such a theology, it is essentially a quiescent one. 'God loves us all', it would say; 'therefore we should love one another. How, then, can we support conflict? Should we not rather urge peace and reconciliation?' In such a theological ethic, social and class conflict have no place.

Sociological and historical factors re-inforced this pattern of response. In a classic study of Methodism in the pit villages of County Durham, published in the early 1970s, it was shown how the effect of nineteenth-century Methodism on the development of working class political consciousness was, at best, ambivalent. Methodism undoubtedly produced leaders among working class people; but the leaders it produced were not of a sort who would articulate class interests as such. 'The beliefs of Methodists did not specifically entail a social outlook which included notions of class interest and conflict. . . . ethical issues were more important than economic or political issues. Furthermore, not only did the saved/unsaved dichotomy cut across social classes . . . but groups in different class positions shared common views of the world, rooted in shared religious beliefs' (1). The effect of Methodism – and the situation in what is now South Yorkshire appears to have been very similar – was to encourage managers and men to work together and to co-operate for what was seen as the common welfare of all. The chapels themselves developed a warm social life where feelings of friendship and communality would be strengthened. Subsequent changes in social, economic and religious circumstances have done little to alter this fundamental orientation.

Nevertheless, even in the mid-1980s there were congregations in and around Barnsley which retained an ethos and a membership notably more 'working class' in character than is to be found in most parts of Britain. Cortonwood, indeed, is a typical example, and it seems that in such congregations there was more sympathy for the miners' cause than in the economically more prosperous and socially more mixed congregations. Even there, however, the support was expressed in the ways we have already described – through financial and other practical assistance, rather than with overt support of the miners' aims.

In so far, then, as there was any perception within the churches of a role for themselves beyond that simply of binding up the wounds, it was a perception expressed in concepts like 'forgiveness' and 'reconciliation', rather than a concern for wider questions of justice and power. The inability to acknowledge openly the presence within the church of people with opposing commitments, however, and the failure to recognise the need to care for and to support them, seriously weakened any possibility there might otherwise have been even of a reconciling role being performed. A fear-borne silence, and a refusal to share fully in the suffering of the community, left the churches isolated and unable to perform even those roles they might have wished to perform. In view of the increasing marginalisation of the churches throughout most of this century, and certainly during the decades since the second world war, this failure was little less than tragic.

The churches were surrounded by turmoil and division. Strongly-held views and radically contradictory emotions were being experienced. Convinced strikers, reluctant strikers, non-strikers; pickets and police; struggling families: all had to live together, and live through the physical, mental and spiritual tensions the dispute produced. Yet within the churches, life continued almost as if nothing was happening. The churches, claiming to be able to offer resources to enable people to live through life's severest trials, in fact offered little more than 'business as usual'. The picture presented was not that of a community of faith, facing joyfully and confidently all that the world has to offer, but rather one of a fearful community, huddling together for self-preservation. Refusing to enter into the conflict, the church abdicated the right to be an agent of reconciliation, let alone a force for justice, once the conflict had run out of the headlines and the pieces had to be put together again.

We do not believe it is now altogether impossible for the churches to gain for themselves a new credibility, although the failure seriously to respond to the strike does make it now more difficult. Yet such response as there was does provide, however inadequately, at least some kind of basis for a new beginning. The statement issued after the end of the strike by the Barnsley Methodist Circuit Meeting was an attempt to express a solidarity with and a support for the people of the area as they strive to create a more positive future both for the mining industry and for the life of their communities:

THE FUTURE OF THE MINING COMMUNITIES

Now that the mining strike is over, this Circuit Meeting, representing 45 Methodist Churches in the Barnsley area:

RECOGNISES the contribution that the mining communities have made to the well-being of our nation;

IS CONVINCED that there is a need for a national energy policy which incorporates a central role for coal;

ACKNOWLEDGES that changes in the mining industry are likely to offer fewer jobs in the future, but

RECOGNISES that any decision on pit closure must take account both of economic and of social factors;

INSISTS that there must be provision for alternative jobs and investments in our communities;

URGES all parties to the dispute to continue to seek a negotiated settlement of the issues that divide them;

BELIEVES that there must be a spirit of forgiveness and reconciliation within our communities if they are to recover;

SUPPORTS continuing measures by people within and outside the churches to give practical help to those suffering financial hardship;

AND COMMENDS to its member-churches a "Check List of Possible Actions" for their consideration as a contribution towards restoring the well-being of our communities.

Appended to the statement was a 'Check-List of Possible Actions' (re-printed at the end of this book). If the churches are prepared not only to issue such statements but also to act upon them, giving serious attention to identifying the real needs of the community and to working with others in a serious programme aimed at meeting the needs, then there may yet be a new future for the churches, in partnership with the people of the battered, struggling yet still undefeated mining communities of Yorkshire.

CHAPTER FOUR

HUNT THE GOSPEL

One Friday evening toward the end of November 1984 the five members of the 'Core Team' of the Barnsley Team Ministry – three ordained Methodist ministers, one full-time and one part-time lay worker – met together to spend a couple of hours studying the Bible. We wanted to reflect theologically upon the significance of the course of the strike, trying to understand a little better what our Christian faith had to say to us as ministers living and working with people whose lives were so dramatically dominated by it.

By an interesting and significant coincidence, two of us, preparing our thoughts in advance of the meeting, had quite independently turned to the same Bible passage: to the strange thirteenth chapter of St Mark's Gospel with its images of woes and judgments, yet with its underlying message of hope in the midst of deep confusion. We were struck by the directness with which it spoke to us.

'When you hear the noise of battle near at hand and the news of battles far away, do not be alarmed. ... You will be handed over to the courts. ... So when you are arrested and taken away, do not worry beforehand what you will say ... Brother will betray brother ... and the father his child; children will turn against their parents ... Impostors will come claiming to be messiahs or prophets ...' (Mk 13:7, 9, 11, 12, 22). Change a few details, and it could almost have been written in Barnsley in 1984.

When things seem to be at their worst, then should we most be filled with hope. That seemed to be the central message of the chapter. If it did nothing else, it was a theme which helped to sustain our preaching during the immediately following season of Advent.

The strike was, undoubtedly, for most people a messy, confused and miserable process. It was a struggle just to keep going. Through it all, too, for many people, there was a sense of futility: 'We know we can't win, but it's a battle we still have to fight'. The cost seemed almost unthinkable. People's life-time savings gone for ever. Many of the things people had come to take for granted – cars, stereos, videos – sold to keep down the level of debt. Families shattered by the stress.

But without struggle, without distress, without persecution, there is no salvation. 'Whoever holds out to the end will be saved' (Mk 13:13). Meanwhile, do not be misled into thinking that the suffering and the confusion are the whole truth. Rather, 'be on your guard ... Be alert, be wakeful. You do not know when the moment (of salvation) comes' (vv 23, 33). Before salvation, however, comes *judgment* (vv 26f). In important ways, the strike represented a time of judgment, when much which had come to be taken for granted was tested and found wanting.

Put to the test and found wanting was a system of industrial relations which had characterised the coal industry since nationalisation in 1947: a system of corporate management in which, particularly through the 1960s and '70s, the NUM had willingly – not to say eagerly – collaborated in the loss of thousands of its members' jobs. The process, however, was one which increasingly tended to drive a wedge between miners and their union structures, and the election of Arthur Scargill as President of the NUM could be seen as an indication that 'enough is enough'.

Until the time of the strike, many miners had been no more than passive members of the union. To a significant extent, this was a direct consequence of the pit-closures of the '60s and '70s. One consequence of the closures was the much greater distances many miners had to travel to work; no longer was the pit at the end of the village street, and fewer and fewer miners were able or willing to give time for union organisation, when to do so would mean attending union meetings sometimes many miles from their homes. The organisation of the union became the task of a small number of activists(1).

If, in electing Scargill as president, the membership of the NUM were declaring that they had had enough of collaboration in the run-down of their industry (Scargill fought his Presidential campaign on the issue of closures), their action co-incided directly with the actions of a government for whom also there could be no continuing class collaboration. One of Margaret Thatcher's chief aims has been to break the consensus which had governed British politics since World War 2, in which – as she believes – the price of trade union collaboration with certain of the aims of the state was that in other and crucial areas they were able to 'hold the country to ransom'.

The conflict between government and miners, however, was but the most visible manifestation of a process which already had been taking place, under governments of varying persuasions, throughout the 1970s. The financing of a welfare state, in which ever greater burdens were being placed on fewer and fewer shoulders, became more and more difficult. Inflation and rising unemployment – the latter in considerable measure a consequence of government policies for dealing with the former – added to the difficulties. The welfare state was undergoing a crisis to which the political Left had no solution. Only the policies of the New Right seemed to offer a sufficiently new approach to solving new problems – the approach of an authoritarian populism determined to revive and to win the battles of class warfare, and to do so by harnessing all the powers of the state machine in a struggle to destroy the chief agency of working class power, the trade unions.

A key element in the post-war welfare state consensus was the promise, based on the expectation of continuous economic expansion, of a corresponding continuous rise in personal living standards. Acceptance of continuing vast inequalities in wealth and income, as well as in access to social provision such as education and health care, was bought by real improvements in standards for almost everyone. So long as the size of the cake was increasing, it seemed to matter less if some still had much bigger slices than others – while the minority who received none of the cake at all could easily be forgotten. For many people, access to cars, to central heating in their homes, to holidays in Spain, to coloured television, came to be taken for granted. So, too, did free health care and schooling.

The crisis of the '70s and '80s, initiated by a dramatic increase in the price of oil, put much of this into question. Spending on social welfare provision could not be sustained and, as levels of unemployment rose, more and more people were excluded from the consumer goods which had come to be expected. For the mining communities of South Yorkshire, the threat of closure of pits brought with it the fear that material benefits, won through years of hard struggle – both physical struggle in the daily round of mining, and industrial struggle through the union – would vanish. At a time when social benefits of all kinds were also being drastically cut, the prospect was intolerable.

For some people, however, the strike itself began to create an awareness that the failure of welfare state capitalism to deliver its promised goods was not its only, nor its most serious, failure. A re-discovery of that communality which has always been at the heart of communities based on occupations like mining – a re-discovery forced upon people as they came more and more to rely upon one another for both material and moral support – led at least a few people to begin to recognise, however dimly, that many of the rewards they had been offered were worth far less than they had supposed. As, one by one, household items were sold off – a stereo here, a video-recorder there – to pay for the more basic necessities – food and clothes – a new scale of values did begin to emerge. 'We thought we could never do without these things, but now we know that sharing and caring for one another are more important': comments like that were often heard in Barnsley toward the end of 1984. A letter received shortly after Christmas from the Women's Support Group in Nottinghamshire said, '... we were greatly encouraged by the fantastic support which came from all over the country to give us a much brighter Christmas than we could hope for. Many of us believe that it was the happiest Christmas we've ever had, because it brought the goodwill and friendship of so many into our homes'.

Thus did judgment begin to merge into salvation. Whereas, over many years, a reliance upon the offerings of consumer-oriented capitalism had come to take the place of mutual support, commitment to home and to nuclear family had slowly undermined solidarity and support for wider family, for friends and for colleagues. The new recognition that this was so went hand-in-hand with a re-discovery of that seam of human warmth and friendship which had always lain not far beneath the surface.

And with salvation, there came, too, a sense of mission. In some ways this was nothing new: the miners have often seen themselves as a vanguard force, fighting battles on behalf of the whole British working class. In the strike, that sense was powerfully re-inforced. Links were forged between the miners and people fighting battle against nuclear power – and nuclear weapons, too. A new awareness grew of the threat of unemployment. The women's groups began to see something at least of the importance of the demands of their feminist sisters. 'We're not just doing this for ourselves', said one miner; 'we're fighting for everyone'.

Through the confusion and untidiness of the strike, therefore, there were signs of hope to be perceived by those alert and wakeful, able to recognise the signs of the times (Mk 13:28). Through the divisiveness which separated miner from miner, police from communities, the NUM from other trade unions, new solidarities were being forged. While much was being judged and found wanting, at the same time new hope was coming to birth, new humanity was being discovered.

The churches need not have been so fearful.

CHAPTER FIVE

WHOSE LAW AND ORDER?

Christian social and political thought has always moved between two poles. On the one hand, there has been an apocalyptic tradition, grounded in biblical passages like Mark 13 and the Book of Revelation, which has been deeply hostile to secular powers and authorities. On the other hand there has been a tradition grounded in Romans 13 and brought to its culmination in the Lutheran doctrine of the 'two realms', which has seen governments as agencies of God within their appointed sphere, to be respected by Christians as divinely instituted. According to this tradition at its most rigorous, any disobedience to legitimately established government is tantamount to disobedience to God himself.

Questions of obedience to the state, and of the limits to the state's authority, became prominent throughout the course of the strike; an increased awareness of civil liberties issues on the part of many people in the mining communities is, perhaps, one of the more hopeful consequences of the strike. If we want to see better policing, as a means of enhancing the stability of communities and protecting freedom for individuals, then we should welcome the critical thinking about police policy and methods which has emerged – even if, more negatively, we cannot ignore the fact that some of the more creative forms of police/public co-operation have been sadly threatened, and some relationships destroyed, as a result of government policies. These things will not easily be restored by enlightened debate, nor even by determined efforts to extend 'community policing'.

There are parts of Britain where suspicion of the police is part of the local folk-culture, but Barnsley before 1984 does not seem to have been such a place. Nevertheless, many local people were profoundly shocked by what they witnessed on the picket lines, on the motorways, in police cells and in the courts. Violence on the picket lines was for several months the main focus of media attention, obscuring not only the main issue of the strike, that of pit closures, but also the real abuses of police power which also took place. Scargill himself may well have regretted the lack of discipline on the part of his own 'troops', and the way this played into the hands of the police,[1] but his own ritual denunciation of 'police violence' when asked to comment on 'the violence' undoubtedly also made it easier for pro-Government propagandists to ignore unprovoked attacks by police on pickets, with violent use of truncheons, horses and riot gear.

One Barnsley miner who had faithfully turned up for picket duty morning after morning, for months on end, finally gave up because, he said, he was sickened by the violence 'on both sides'. 'I never expected to see a baton charge down an English country lane', he added; 'my attitude to the police has to be different from now on'. He had become disheartened, he said, by the way in which it was impossible to move across the countryside without the police knowing all the time where you were.

The obvious visibility of a heavy police presence on the county's motorways had a distinctive effect on public perceptions and attitudes. South Yorkshire has a friendly 'feel' to it as a place to live and work, and a high value is set on freedom to move around: the cheap fares policy means that people in an area of relatively low car ownership can travel from Barnsley to places like Sheffield, Leeds or Doncaster by public transport without having to worry about cost, while car drivers are grateful for motorways which are rarely subject to major hold-ups. It came, therefore, as a shock to South Yorkshire people to find road blocks set up at motorway junctions, where drivers and passengers were questioned about their identity and destination. Ordinary citizens had their freedom of movement curtailed at great inconvenience.

The sense of being watched at every turn was not confined to miners. On the motorways there were convoys of police transit vans, while conglomerations of assorted police vehicles were often to be seen parked on the motorway bridges. Sheffield Policewatch report:

> 'We have seen ordinary members of the public attempting to go to work turned back at the roadblocks because the police are claiming that a large number of miners are causing a disturbance. On checking we have found just a handful of peaceful pickets and no disturbance'.[2]

At the other end of the scale, there was the strange spectacle of solitary police officers keeping a lonely vigil on obscure country lanes at South Yorkshire's border with Nottinghamshire. The county boundary began to feel like the frontier of a police state.

As the strike progressed, there was increasing evidence that the local police were making an effort to counter the deterioration in relationships between police and public. Instructions were issued to ensure that arrests were made by members of visiting forces rather than by South Yorkshire officers. There were moves to extend the relatively undeveloped community policing practices. By the end of the strike, the high profile tactics had all but ceased, and police visibility became a matter of seeing more constables walking the streets.

Yet in the mining communities, there remains in many quarters a deep suspicion, and even hatred, of the police; there is evidence of police officers who have moved house because of pressure brought to bear on their families, and particularly on their children. Games of 'police and pickets' in school playgrounds may quickly disappear, but the feeling of many South Yorkshire children that the police are basically against them will no doubt persist.

Paradoxically, alongside these feelings, there is also among many people a recognition that individual police officers are not really to blame for what has happened, but that many of them have been victims themselves of government policies and strategies. They have, of course, received financial compensation in the form of overtime payments, at a time when miners were subject to severe financial penalties, but there was nevertheless real pain borne by policemen and by their families. Days and nights of overtime severely disrupted family life. Real physical injuries were sustained, even if peaceful picketing was the norm at most pits.

Some members of the police were forced to move house because of the attitudes of neighbours – often, neighbours for whose plight they themselves had much sympathy. Few would not themselves have had friends or relatives among the striking miners, yet some have been obliged to give up drinking in their local pubs – an apparently trivial penalty, although the isolation of police officers from their communities in fact constitutes a serious development which could in the end reinforce the more destructive forms of policing.

The alienation from the police engendered by the policing of the strike will not have been in any way lessened by recent reports of court proceedings. The Sheffield *Morning Telegraph* (June 14 1985) reported that PC Fred Browning of Merseyside police, giving evidence at the trial of miners arrested at Orgreave on June 18 1984, admitted that his statement contained serious inaccuracies, and was not in fact his own account of the arrest he had made.

'A plain-clothes detective gave a rough résumé of what he wanted written in the statement', PC Browning was quoted as saying. 'We just wrote out what we were told'. Such reports will do nothing to undermine the scepticism of at least one Barnsley miner about charges made the day he was arrested – exactly 55 people charged with riotous assembly, and another 55 with unlawful assembly. He is convinced the charge sheets had been typed up the night before the disturbance took place.

His scepticism seemed to be vindicated when all the charges were in fact dropped. The Chief Constable of South Yorkshire rather lamely suggested that there were difficulties in getting people to remember accurately what had happened in June 1984.

The same man believes, however, that the worst police atrocities were committed by officers from non-mining areas; he saw a clear difference between the approach of members of South Wales forces and men from London and Birmingham. From his own colliery, he reports highly provocative actions like throwing loose change in front of pickets; he also tells of a pneumaconiosis sufferer being told that his walking stick was an offensive weapon. Meanwhile, the more cautious interim report of the NCCL's independent inquiry refers to provocative actions such as the rhythmic banging of riot shields, apparently arbitrary arrests, and the waving of pay packets at pickets.(3)

The NCCL report suggests that the remarkably high proportion of arrests not followed by preferment of charges (17%) indicates the use of arrest procedures to remove people from the scene of trouble and thus to reduce the effectiveness of picketing; a report in *The Guardian* (March 18 1985) suggested that magistrates used bail conditions in a similar way, and concluded that 'the law appears to have been used as a means of social control rather than for its intended purposes'.

The NCCL report cites the use of between 1,000 and 2,000 police officers to accompany the first Cortonwood striker who returned to work.(4) Overkill of this sort inevitably leads to public disorder; but the apparently limitless supply of police resources could only have been possible as a result of political decisions. The Energy Secretary, Peter Walker, insisted that coal should continue to be produced in Nottinghamshire and, much to the distress of some senior police officers, police were used to ensure that this objective was met.

One among a number of understandings of the proper role of governments in human society is that they should perform the 'neutral' role of attempting to reconcile the conflicting interests which make up the life of a nation; that they should seek to stand above the conflict of particular and partial interests, and to articulate and represent a broad common interest on behalf of the people they are elected to serve. This idealist understanding of government has almost certainly never been achieved in practice, and it is quite clear that in the case of the coal strike there was no attempt to achieve it. Government was set to defeat the miners, and was prepared to use every means available. Police, law and law-courts were all co-opted to support the interests, not of the state and its people, but of a government committed to the defeat of miners and their union.

At a quite early stage in the dispute there were stories circulating in South Yorkshire, as elsewhere, about 'troops in police uniforms'. These stories were almost impossible to substantiate, and most of them are now widely recognised as having emanated from *News Line,* the newspaper of the Revolutionary Workers' Party.

A common element in these stories was the presence on picket lines of officers in unnumbered blue overalls. Whether or not troops were deployed, there do seem to have been numerous occasions when identification of individual officers has been impossible. However, even if there was some truth in these accounts and a limited number of military personnel were deployed, perhaps experimentally, this should not be allowed to shift attention from the much more central issue of the use of police in para-military fashion under national political control.

The first Special Patrol Group in the UK was established by the Metropolitan Police in 1965, and since then 'instant response units' under various names have been set up in each constabulary area. Members of these units are trained in riot control and the use of firearms. They are provided with similar equipment and identical transport – the now familiar white Transit vans. It is difficult not to see this combined force of more than 10,000 officers as a 'third force' of riot police, straddling the roles of both constabulary and military and rendering unnecessary the need to bring in troops if a government wishes coercively to enforce its will against some 'enemy within'.

Since 1964, control of police forces in Britain has been shared three ways between police authorities, chief constables and the Home Secretary. Machinery has also been developed, however, to by-pass this tripartite arrangement, making political control possible through the agency of the Association of Chief Police Officers (ACPO) and the National Reporting Centre (NRC). Ironically, ACPO originally came into being in order to increase the autonomy of senior police officers from the Home Office; yet, while it has established a right to act unchallenged by government or by police authorities, it is also, at least in relation to its role within the NRC, directly responsible to the Home Office.

The NRC was conceived at a meeting of ACPO with senior Home Office officials in April 1972, in the aftermath of Scargill's success in closing the Saltley coke depot. Portrayed as an administrative link to make mutual aid between different police forces more efficient, the Centre was first activated in response to NUM activities in February 1974, when it operated for twenty-five days. It was not used at all during the period of the 1974-79 Labour Government, and then was used only sporadically until the 1984-5 dispute, which was far and away the biggest operation with which it has been involved. Several commentators have insisted that it is an undeclared command centre of a national police force, and that through it the Home Secretary can give political direction to police operations.

Some, indeed, have gone further than this, seeing the use of police and courts during the strike to enforce government policies, sometimes with dubious legality, as one among a number of indications that Britain has become, or is on the way to becoming, a 'police state'. Other indications are such things as the considerable extension of police powers through the Police and Criminal Evidence Act, the forcible removal of people from peace camps and the prevention of assemblies (as at Stonehenge in June 1985), suspicion of the widespread use of telephone tapping, the prosecutions of Sarah Tisdall and Clive Ponting, and so on.

The term 'police state' is not in fact clearly defined, although it is certainly the case that some important liberties – not least a continuing media pluralism, reflected particularly in regional newspapers, in some of the output of local radio stations, and in the continuing freedom to publish critical books, pamphlets and articles – still exist in Britain in ways not to be found in most countries to which the term 'police state' is applied. On the other hand, the restrictions on peaceful picketing and on freedom of movement, policies of arbitrary arrest, police assaults on members of the public, special branch surveillance of trade unionists, the manufacturing of evidence, the misuse of bail conditions, and so forth, all give cause for very great concern.

'Every person', wrote St Paul, 'must submit to the supreme authorities' (Rom 13:1). The experience of many miners and their supporters during the strike was that they had little choice but to submit, and undoubtedly the response of many people – including many Christians, both within and beyond the coalfields – was along the lines of 'Thank goodness someone is prepared to show them who's the boss!'

Yet the tradition of resistance to unjust and unreasonable laws is a long and honourable one. Many of the basic rights we take for granted were won only after long struggles. Law can protect freedom; it can also institutionalise injustice and oppression. Christians, in particular, need to ponder deeply and seriously the way in which Jesus came into direct conflict with the legal authorities of his own society, and seems frequently to have launched vigorous tirades against them: perhaps the twenty-third chapter of St Matthew's Gospel is the most striking example. Probably, however, no New Testament figure has more powerful things to say about the impotence of laws to create justice than has St Paul.

In the Letter to the Romans, Paul's central concern is to explain how, against all Jewish expectation, God has established justice in the world *without a dependence upon law.* Law, indeed, achieves the ultimate injustice: the law of Judaism and the law of Rome together decree the death of Jesus, the one just person! 'But now, quite independently of the Law, God's justice has been brought to light' (Rom 3:21).

Why, then, later in the same letter, does Paul speak of the duty of 'submission to the supreme authorities'? We need to read his words carefully, and in their context. When Paul was writing, the Roman Empire had not yet appeared as a persecutor of the church. Administration was in the hands of Seneca, who gave the Empire probably its best ever period of government. Paul is writing about that particular government, not about any and every government there might be.

Then, we need to note exactly what he says. 'Every person must *submit* to the supreme authorities'. He speaks of respect, but not of collaboration, attachment, affection or love. Our attitude to the state should be positive, but not therefore uncritical; and most certainly he does not envisage what has often happened in Christian history when the church has taken over the functions of an official state religion.

Again, we should note how he describes the 'authorities'. 'They are God's agents', he says, 'working for your good' (13:4); that is why we need have 'no fear' of them. But suppose they cease to work for our good? Suppose they threaten arbitrarily to close down the only place where we can earn our living? Suppose they use their agents to imprison us, threaten us, attack us, for no reason other than that we are determined to struggle for our right to work, for the future of our families and our communities? Then – by Paul's own logic – the authorities have deserted the task for which they were established by God, and the argument for submission can no longer apply.

Most importantly, we should be aware of the motive which for Paul underlies the call to 'submit'. When Paul looks at the realities of his own world, he sees in those realities the will of the Creator at work; that is why he says 'we must be subject'. But in saying that, his real concern is to call the Christian to take a stand before God, and thus to enter into the possibility of genuine service of God in every-day life. What is at stake in everything Paul writes is the matter of Christian freedom, which for Paul is always the freedom which knows itself called to serve God. We submit to earthly realities, including the power of the state, not merely to acquiesce in things as they are, but rather to take our part in the transformation of the world which is God's will. (5)

One of the most important lessons to be learned from the policing of the strike is the way people's attitudes to 'the law' can be changed. Not only have miners and their women folk come to a much more sophisticated understanding of the police than they possessed before the strike; the churches, too, have begun seriously to debate issues of civil disobedience. The Bishop of Durham has recently begun to speak of the need for a 'liberation theology' for Britain, earthing his very moderate assertions in some of the issues raised by the strike.

The essence of liberation theology is that it is born out of real experience, as people look for gospel sustenance in their struggle against oppressive forces. Conservative people (like Oscar Romero in El Salvador, or Helder Camara in Brazil) have found themselves driven to radical action as they have come to recognise that oppressive forces which destroy people's lives and freedom cannot be reconciled with God's will.

It is not simply in response to the rhetoric of Arthur Scargill that men and women in very traditional and peaceful South Yorkshire have been driven to challenge the authority of the police: people have taken risks in the face of massive military-style police deployment because of what they have seen happening to their colleagues and neighbours and communities. They have also seen the possibility of what can happen when you are confident of the support of others around you.

If it is in his Letter to the Romans that St Paul writes most powerfully about the limitations of law in ordering human life, it is probably in his correspondence with the Christians in Corinth that he most vigorously presents his alternative vision – that of a community, drawn together in spite of social and economic divisions by the power of God's Spirit; a community in which special importance is accorded to those normally thought of as 'weak'. Recently, it has been shown that when Paul in the Corinthian letters writes about the 'weak' and the 'strong' (e.g. in 1 Cor 8), he is referring to those respectively of low and of high social status, who also of course are respectively poor and wealthy.[(6)] Paul's message, however, is not just a bland message that they must learn to live with one another. It is that, in cases of conflict, *the rights of the 'weak' and poor must have precedence over those of the 'strong' and wealthy*; 'those parts of the body which we regard as less honourable', he adds (1 Cor 12:23), 'are treated with special honour'.

There is significance in the fact that people in the mining communities became aware of the inadequacies of 'law and order' at the same time that they were also discovering the possibility of developing new ways of living together with one another. The support they gave to one another during the strike, they realised, did not depend on any externally-imposed framework of law. St Paul's understanding of the limitations of the power of law, coupled with what he has to say about fellowship and community, offers a Christian framework for understanding what has been happening on the picket lines and in the courts during the strike.

CHAPTER SIX

STRUGGLE

At the centre of the coal strike, there were people. Struggling people, suffering people, disillusioned people, hopeful people. Perhaps above all, people who were being transformed, in one direction or another. Many people, because of the strike, are different now from the way they were before it.

Scenes of violence, police convoys, arrests, talks between the Coal Board and the Union: these, throughout the strike, were at the centre of the media reports; but behind such sensational events which are of the essence of journalism, the fundamental fact for a town like Barnsley was that one third of its male population were on strike. The events which hit the headlines and which were available for all the world to see were no more than the tip of a vast iceberg of personal struggle for survival.

From the early days of the strike, it became clear that the NCB would have to deal not only directly with their own workforce, but also with the deeper roots of the miners in the total life of whole communities where mining had been a way of life for generations, where fathers had been followed by sons, and they in turn by grandsons and great-grandsons, all in their turn working in the mines, and at the same time forming closely-knit communities which had faced hardship before and would, if necessary, face it again; people prepared to confront what had become a threat to their whole way of life. The strike was not just about jobs, it was about survival. Very quickly it became a war in which a total population was engaged, and which took over almost everything else in importance and in its effects.

In an area where miners gave solid support to the strike almost to the end, the consequences for different people varied enormously. Perhaps a major difference was between those who actively supported the strike, and those who, while they were unwilling positively to give their support, nevertheless were still unwilling to show disloyalty to their union, their families and their community.

For those who actively supported the strike, there was a camaraderie, a constant activity of picket line duty, of travelling the length and breadth of the country to gain support for their action. For many of the wives, there was the work of staffing the food kitchens to ensure that their families received at least one hot meal a day. There were the many activities of the women's support groups. Such dedicated action gave a united strength and support which made it possible to face the hardships. Friendships developed, determination increased. As days and weeks went by, and food parcels and donations arrived literally from all over the world, morale was kept high.

Many, however, were involved in none of this activity. For them, even more than for those who were active, life became an almost impossible struggle. Tension in families increased as time went by. Lack of money caused increasing stress. The local Marriage Guidance Council reports that the divorce rate rose sharply during this period.

The fact that many families were dependent upon a weekly income of only £14.00 (later reduced to £13.00) could not but create stress. Savings were soon spent. As time went by there was increasing need for such items as new clothes for ever-growing children, and by the time that Christmas approached the need for support from the community was intense. Both the media and the Coal Board expected that this would be the breaking point and for some, enticed also by the promises of cash from the Coal Board, it was so. The majority, however, continued to give one another support and encouragement, while further gifts from around the world served to boost morale again. One woman tells how she was reduced to tears when her seven-year-old son told her not to worry about Christmas – but please, he asked, could he have a new battery for one of his toys?

Children, indeed, responded to the situation with as much determination and grit as their parents. The reflection of parental attitudes, however, was often noted by school teachers. Fighting in school, accompanied with messages of 'That's from my Dad to yours', became more common as bitterness increased toward those not actively supporting the strike.

Feelings of frustration and isolation were common. People were in a situation they seemed powerless to control, in desperate financial straits, uncertain whom they could trust and in whom they could confide. One man tells how, having decided that he had no option but to return to work, he nevertheless went to his local Branch meeting, where Arthur Scargill was speaking. An hour later, he came out again, determined to stay on strike; yet twenty-four hours later still he was saying to himself, 'I can't believe how I swallowed such a pack of lies'. Such constant swinging of emotions was almost impossible for many to cope with.

Miners and their families were not the only ones, however, to be affected by the strike. Effects were evident upon the community as a whole. The ambivalence of attitudes toward the police, and the effects upon members of the police force themselves, we have already described: months after the end of the strike, the tension remains. At the same time, crime increased dramatically during the strike – crimes in general by twenty-six per cent, and burglary by thirty-six per cent.

The economic effects upon the community were also very marked: well over £2 million were being lost in wages every week. The effect of this was most significant in many of the villages, where miners constituted fifty per cent of the employed population or more. The drop in trade was reported to be between twenty-five and forty per cent. Many shops were forced to close, while others saw gains made over a life-time disappear.

One small butcher tells of how his life-time savings were lost during the strike. He sees no way in which, at his present stage of life, he can ever make up the loss. Another couple, a few months before the strike, sold their home and put their savings into a fish and chip business. They, too, lost everything. Meanwhile, larger ventures like the well-established Albert Hirst chain of butchers shops, which normally had supplied the pit canteens, were reduced to a market stall; Brian Barnard, fruiterers and florists, suffered the same experience, and Barnsley's long-established jewellers, Benjamin Harral, also ceased trading.

For these, as for many others, the end of the strike by no means brought an end to the problems. In many cases, jobs have been lost permanently. At one stage, twelve shops were for sale in one of Barnsley's small satellite townships, and although the Small Business Association has repeatedly approached the government for compensation for small businesses, the cries have been unheeded. Those businesses which have survived will be slow to take on staff again, and this in turn affects programmes like the Youth Training Scheme, where placements for some teenagers cannot be found because businesses have no work for them to do.

In the service sector, everything came to a halt. House prices were static, or in some cases fell as mortgages were not available to miners. Insurance was something miners managed without; many cancelled their life and savings policies in order to have a little more cash in their pockets. As retail traders offered what support they could in the form of discounts to striking miners, so service-sector businesses also did whatever was possible: mortgage re-payments were usually waived until the end of the strike; some insurance brokers offered to pay insurance premiums in certain cases. The hope was that such support would be recognised and honoured once the strike was over.

Few people in Barnsley can entirely have escaped the effects of the strike. The town became a place of great need, materially, psychologically and spiritually. Some were prevented by the 'political' overtones of the strike from responding to that need; yet help, from within the community itself as well as from far beyond, did materialise. Barnsley Metropolitan District Council alone spent over £2.7 million in food vouchers and rebates of various kinds.

In the aftermath, many divisions remain. As the pressure became too great for some, and they began to return to work, there were scenes of parents weeping in disbelief at their sons' return to work. Brothers vowed never again to speak to one another. Neighbours rejected each other. The anger, bitterness and even hatred has left deep scars, which will not quickly heal. Indeed, those who worked in the General Strike of 1926 are still sometimes referred to as 'scabs', such is the strength of feelings aroused at such times.

One of the most perceptive of Christian theologians in our time, Jürgen Moltmann, has written these words:

> The power of hope is only manifested in the crisis of progress today if it leads to life even in the face of deadly crisis. In confrontation with the economic, political and ecological processes that are taking place, it must make people ready to act in time and to make the necessary sacrifices. There will be no survival for mankind [sic] without the rebirth of the power of hope ... the rediscovery of the capacity for suffering is part of the will to live and the power of hope.(1)

'Life even in the face of deadly crisis' ... 'ready to act in time and to make the necessary sacrifices' ... 'rediscovery of the capacity for suffering': phrases of that sort, expressing themes which are at the heart of the Christian gospel, come immediately to mind when we reflect on the experiences of the people of the mining communities. In a world which too often overcomes its hunger by letting others go hungry, which overcomes its oppression by enslaving others, the people of the mining communities glimpsed at least a little of the gospel truth, that suffering and sacrifice could be borne, as part of the human struggle to make and to keep the world both human and humane.

At the centre of New Testament Christianity stands the proclamation of salvation through the suffering and death of Jesus. But Jesus does not suffer alone, and, if Jesus suffers, then there is hope too for those who suffer with him. According at least to St Luke's Gospel, the freedom fighter who suffers beside him also is received into 'paradise' (Lk 24:43). Previously, Jesus has already made it clear that only those who are willing themselves to 'take up their cross' in solidarity with him and with one another can be his disciples (Lk 9:23-26). Time after time, the church has failed to hear and to obey that call; yet if within the mining communities there are even a few people who have experienced for themselves anything of the possibility or the reality of redemption through suffering, then the need for a church which will continue to witness to the eternal value of such experiences becomes even greater.

In the weeks and months following the strike, the feeling of many people has been one of 'Thank goodness it's all over. Let's forget it, put it behind us, and try to get back to normality again'. It is hardly surprising that people should feel so. Yet if the strike is forgotten, there seems a real likelihood that the important lessons learned from it will be forgotten, too.

An unwillingness to forget the past – indeed, its constant repetition and re-affirmation through the telling and re-telling of stories – is an essential element in Christian faith. Above all, Christians repeat time after time the central story of the world's redemption through the suffering, death and resurrection of Jesus; but we also tell many other stories, too, from the myths of the early chapters of Genesis, to the stories of Christian heroines and heroes of our own century. Perhaps a proper role of the church in the mining communities is that of not allowing the story to be forgotten, reminding people of a past they might prefer to forget, by telling the story ourselves, and by prompting and encouraging others to do the same – in words, in picture, in song, in drama, in film, and in whatever other ways may be devised.

But telling the story alone is not enough. From the very earliest days of the church, when people told the story of Jesus they told it in particular ways and for particular purposes. They told the story to inspire faith and hope and love. They told it to make it clear that the suffering at the heart of the story was not blind and pointless, but that it had indeed no less than an eternal significance.

The story of the coal strike needs to be told in such a way that those who lived through it and suffered through it may come to see that their sufferings, too, have a part to play in the world's redemption. If the church does not tell the story that way, is there anyone else who will?

CHAPTER SEVEN

WOMEN

'The decision of the Yorkshire miners to strike in defence of their jobs and their industry has raised strong feelings in the Barnsley area. We, as women, would like to express our support for the strike action and to highlight some of the issues involved.

If pits are closed on grounds other than exhaustion, then the employment prospects for local people will be bleak indeed. Any jobs that go now mean that our youngsters will face only the dole-queue in the future. The latest attempt by the NCB to buy off jobs is geared to weaken the Miners' Union. We think that the thousands of pounds now being offered would be better spent in preserving jobs and keeping pits open.

We realise that miners and their families will endure hardships during the strike and that no-one relishes the prospect of mounting bills. However, those same sacrifices were made by our forefathers who gave their lives to the industry and struggled to protect jobs and improve conditions. Let us take their example and stand firmly together to ensure the future of our community.

Finally we wish to object to the assumption made in some sections of the popular press that all miners' wives oppose the decision to strike. We suspect that the vast majority of miners' families realise that the only other alternative is to bury our heads in the sand and hope that our pit won't be next.'

This letter,(1) with an invitation to like-minded women to join together, was printed in the *Barnsley Chronicle* following a meeting on Sunday 11 March 1984, when a group of five women met in Joan Davidson's front room to discuss how they could express their support for the strike. Anger was the emotion that roused the women to organise. Anger because the media were depicting them as against the strike. Anger at being portrayed as the victims of irresponsible action by the NUM. Anger at being disregarded as a political force.

The women who wrote the letter and submitted it to the *Chronicle* didn't really expect it to be printed. Within a matter of days, however, their numbers had risen to two dozen and the movement was under way. It is impossible to say how many women became involved. The initial group grew and became known as Barnsley Women Against Pit Closures. This group was open to any women who supported the strike, and several who were involved had links with Northern College. Later in 1984 a group known as Barnsley Miners' Wives organised themselves, many having been involved with the initial group. Both Women Against Pit Closures and Barnsley Miners' Wives were made up of smaller groups established in each mining community. Representatives from each met together on a weekly basis and maintained regular telephone contact with each other.

Who are these women who became angry and, because of it, organised themselves in support of their men? Mostly, they are women from mining families, many with both husband and sons down the pit.

Most, until 1984, centred their lives around housework and their families. They were the ones in the household who always did the cooking and the housework, cared for the family, more than likely stayed in most nights whilst their husbands went for a drink with the lads and, when they did go out, probably went with their husbands to the Miners' Welfare. They are women who are proud of their men, their children, their homes, the fact that they come from a mining community. Many would ask permission of their husbands before arranging to go out with the girls; voted Labour without really knowing why; had heard of feminism and Greenham Common, but saw both as having very little relevance to themselves.

On the whole most would say they were happy with their lot; the life they led was the one, with a few material improvements, that their mothers and grandmothers had led. If they weren't happy, most believed they had no right to complain: after all, their standard of living wasn't bad, and since the '70's many miners were buying their own houses. They had been born and grown up in a community where 'the focus on men and masculinity is more pronounced than most. Apart from the fact that strength is held in high esteem, the cultural activity of the community revolves predominantly around men'. [2]

Among them was Ann Scargill. Her involvement in the Groups is seen by many to be opportunism, but in reality she neither sought nor welcomed publicity. As she sees it, her involvement was that of any miner's wife. Certainly, the women in the Groups speak of her with great warmth and affection. She is an important part of the Women's Groups and they are at pains to defend and protect her from unwanted publicity.

The Role of the Women

'Close a pit, kill a Community'. That clear and concise message says why women had a place in the 1984/5 coal strike. They insisted on the right to fight alongside the miners, against pit closures and for the future of their community, themselves and their children. They were locked into a fight with the Government and many saw the strike as not just for the miners and their communities but 'for all the working class, if they would just realise it'.

The first few weeks of the strike saw most miners' families living off their savings. It wasn't long, however, before the women realised that one of the most important ways of supporting the miners would be to organise food kitchens. In areas where facilities could not be found, miners received food parcels and vouchers.

This aspect of their role in the strike probably received most publicity. Some of the women are upset by references to 'Soup Kitchens'; they are proud of the fact that whenever possible full meals were served. The women not only organised the cooking and serving of the food, they also found the premises, raised funds and organised collections of food to be served at the kitchens. Some local butchers, grocers, bakers, provided free food, but at the end of the day what was served at the kitchens depended on what was available.

At first only miners went for meals, but gradually whole families went, and soon the kitchens were providing the main meal, each day, for miners and their families. The kitchens became the hub of the new, more closely knit communities, and served not only to feed people but also to keep up morale. At Christmas the groups organised parties for the children and ensured that each miner received a chicken, a £5 food voucher and two tins of Irish butter.

As the strike progressed, the financial situation gradually worsened. Single miners received no state benefit and had to rely on others for money. Married miners were treated as single, their wives claiming their own entitlement – which was reduced at first by £15, and then by £16, that being the amount the Government 'assumed' was being paid in strike pay. Most families, i.e. husband, wife and 2 children, received in the region of £14 or, later, £13 a week to live on. Marsha Marshall felt that the most helpful area in which she was involved was Welfare Benefits advice. 'It enabled women and men to realise that they were not alone', says Marsha. 'There's a pain barrier. Once through, they coped'. For working class people, the shame of not being able to pay the mortgage, gas, electricity, telephone bills was real, and certainly in the early days added to the pressure on the families. The women's groups were able to put pressure on the YEB to reduce the payments from £7 to 50p-£1 a week.

The women's groups were also involved in collecting and redistributing children's clothing, and especially baby and maternity clothing. Eventually the DHSS agreed to make payments to provide baby clothing a week before the baby was due, but many were born while their parents had no clothing for them.

The importance of mutual support, morale-boosting and the sharing of problems, cannot be underestimated. Had this role not been performed, many more men would have returned to work as tensions within their families increased. To this extent, what one could call the more traditional female roles were the most important in prolonging the strike; yet these traditional roles were carried out in non-traditional ways which owed much to the organisation of the Women's Groups and to the ability and willingness of the women to take responsibility, to go out, to acquire knowledge and to become the focus for action and advice.

Money was essential to establish and maintain the food kitchens, food parcels and vouchers. The women in Barnsley refused money from the NUM because they believed it was their job to support the Union, not to drain it. Money was raised in every conceivable way. They organised pie-'n'-pea suppers, jumble sales, sponsored fancy dress pub crawls, coffee mornings, sponsored walks, autumn fares, bingo sessions, discos, and much more. They published and sold literature. They travelled the country and stood on street corners and at factory gates shaking tins and buckets at passers by. They became guest speakers at public meetings and appealed for funds. They went on TV and local radio. They travelled abroad, speaking at union rallies and public meetings. They were overwhelmed by the warmth and generosity of people in Britain, Ireland, Italy, France, Germany, Belgium, Yugoslavia and elsewhere. They were interviewed by reporters from all over the world, and donations and offers of holidays for children poured in. Money was received, often weekly, from people all over Britain especially from pensioners, and their sense of gratitude and indebtedness is overwhelming. The women know how hard and bitter the struggle has been, and how much harder and more bitter it would have been without the financial and moral support they have received.

Picketing and Demonstrations

Probably the most contentious moment, and for the men the most threatening, at least at first, was when the women decided to picket the working miners. Lorraine Bowler in her speech at the National Women's rally in May 1984 (3), said:

> This fight does not just belong to the men, it belongs to us all. It has been good over the weeks to compare how some men reacted to women's involvement at the beginning and how they react now. It has been a gradual acceptance for the most. The reception we receive from the men on the picket lines and demonstrations is tremendous. I believe that if you shout long enough people will begin to listen to what you have to say. I am going to shout long and loud enough to make sure they do listen. Men and women should work together. We ought to be one voice as a working class movement shouting at the Government and MacGregor.
>
> At the beginning of the strike women from the Barnsley group wanted to go picketing and were told that it was a bad enough job organising the men. All I can say to that is, women do not need anyone to organise them. They can organise themselves. The proof of that is shown in this hall today.
>
> I'm sure that for some or most of the women here today, it is the same in their homes as it has been in mine over the weeks. There are arguments now as to whose turn it is to babysit. Talk about job sharing! We've seen it at its best over the past eight or nine weeks.
>
> Being active, as we are, takes away most of the uncertainty that is involved in a strike . . .

Not all women in the groups went picketing. Those who went did so because the strike was about their future, and they believed it was both their right and their duty to be with the miners on the picket lines. They tell of working miners who were prepared to pass other picketing miners, but who would not go past women pickets. They tell of being terrified by the attitude of the police; of the police being just as violent toward women as toward men – something which shocked the miners as much as, if not more than, it shocked their wives. They also tell of the comradeship which evolved between women and men on the picket lines, and between those who were arrested and appeared in court.

In an attempt to show how much support there was for the miners, and to give emotional support to the women who were involved in the women's groups, the Barnsley group decided to hold a National Women's Rally in Barnsley. It took place on May 12th, 1984. They had never before been involved in organising such an event. They expected perhaps 2,000 women to march through Barnsley and to congregate inside and outside the Civic Hall. In the event, 10,000 came – an indication of the strength of the women's movement within the coalfields and of their support for the strike.

A few weeks later, on July 22nd, miners' wives and other women supporters representing every coalfield in Britain met at Northern College, Barnsley, in a National Conference. The aim was to organise a National Women's Demonstration, which eventually took place on August 11th, when 25,000 women demonstrated in London. Its purpose was to highlight the support women were giving to the miners, and to inform the public at large of the effects that pit closures would have on mining communities.

The Other Women

The Women's Support Groups, of course, were made up only of a minority of women from the mining communities; there were many more who never became involved in the groups. Why was that so?

Certainly not because a majority of miners' wives were against the strike. In reality, few were, although those involved in the groups find it difficult to believe that most of the miners who went back to work would have betrayed their workmates in that way if their wives had not put pressure upon them. Some women not involved in the groups, on the other hand, were themselves in employment; it was their earnings which often made it possible for husbands and other male relatives to stay on strike.

The women not involved in the groups have generally not been vocal about their feelings. Because they are less easily identifiable than those of the women who were involved, it is not easy to say why they remained outside the organised fellowship of other women. Nevertheless, some reasons seem clear.

First, the women's groups were seen as a political force in favour of the strike and encouraging it to be prolonged. They were not merely about helping people to cope with its effects. Given that many people's support for the strike was less than total, it is not surprising that women from families where support for the strike was only lukewarm tended not to be involved. One determining factor, therefore, may have been the degree of involvement of different men in the strike, and, perhaps more significantly, whether the menfolk were on strike because they believed in it or merely because they were not prepared to be seen to act against the union.

Secondly, however, many women whose menfolk were active in the strike would not have been encouraged to become involved. One consequence of involvement in the groups was that, in an area where child care is still very much 'women's work', the men found themselves having to look after children. Barnsley has been one of those places where the women's movement happened elsewhere. The politicisation and organisation of women, their demand for recognition and their grasping of power would seem threatening both to men and to women. Many women could not see that they had any right to be involved; nor could many men, some of whom expressly refused permission to their wives to join the women's groups.

Again, there was a problem for many women of 'image'. They saw little in the groups to which they could easily relate. How much this was due to the negative media image of loud-mouthed, militant working class women, and how much to gradual changes which have taken place in mining communities is hard to say. Certainly, many miners' families no longer see the Miners' Welfare as the social centre of the community. Home ownership, holidays abroad, possession of stereo, colour TV and video recorder, have led many to see their lives in wider terms. The Miners' Welfare may have been the obvious place for the women's groups to meet, to organise their canteens, and so on; but for women who were not used to going there, who perhaps even 'looked down' on it, the image both of the institute and of the group which met there was a severe obstacle. Not even the provision of meals there was sufficient to break down this antipathy: it was by no means unknown for miners to go for their meals, leaving their wives and children to eat at home. Many women, therefore, remained isolated both physically and socially from the groups and from other miners' wives, and many felt intimidated by the fervour and emotion which they perceived within the groups.

Whether or not the women were involved in the women's groups, life for those who lived through the strike will certainly not be the same again.

Coping with mounting bills, no luxuries, no heating, little food, depression, frustration, lack of power over their own lives, and with having their menfolk at home instead of at work, created stresses which affected even the strongest of individuals and of relationships. One of the major benefits for those in the women's groups was the strength they gained from each other. Those not in the groups had the same problems to cope with. Some were lucky enough to have a good support network of their own family and friends. Others had little support, and just struggled.

A transfiguration

To leap from the story of women and the coal strike to the pages of the New Testament may seem a long jump indeed. Yet, in a world where 'nothing is as it seems' – as Alice discovered in Wonderland – it is no bad thing to try a few unexpected leaps, to see where they may take us.

Something over a decade ago, in a book called *The Transfiguration of Politics,* the American theologian Paul Lehmann pointed to the New Testament story of the transfiguration of Jesus (Mt 17:1-8; see also Mk 9:2-8, Lk 9:28-36) as a key to an understanding of the political realities of our own time.[4] Let us try the leap, then, from the story of women in Barnsley to this particular episode in the gospels.

> Jesus began to make it clear to his disciples that he had to go to Jerusalem, and there to suffer much from the elders, chief priests, and doctors of the law; to be put to death and to be raised again on the third day . . .
>
> Six days later (or, 'About eight days after this conversation': Lk 9:28) Jesus took Peter and James and John the brother of James, and led them up a high mountain where they were alone; and in their presence he was transfigured; his face shone like the sun, and his clothes became white as the light. And they saw Moses and Elijah appear, conversing with him. . . . (Lk 9:31 adds that they 'spoke of his departure, the destiny he was to fulfil in Jerusalem').
>
> When they returned to the crowd, a man came up to Jesus, fell on his knees before him, and said, 'Have pity, sir, on my son: he is an epileptic and has bad fits . . .'. (Mt 16:21, 17:1-3, 14-15).

The context of the story is important. Jesus has just announced his intention to challenge the power structures of the world – 'the elders, chief priests and doctors of the law'. Yet, rather than proceeding to Jerusalem to do so, he instead takes his friends on a mountain-climbing expedition. The story of what then took place is filled with biblical symbolism.

First, the transfiguration occurs, according to Mark and Matthew, 'six days later' than the prediction of the passion; that is to say, on the seventh day thereafter. Undoubtedly here there is a reference to the Jewish understanding of the importance of the sabbath – the seventh day of the week. For the Hebrews, the cycle of each week was linked to the myths of creation in the Book of Genesis. In later Judaism, the whole history of the world was similarly divided into seven, concluding with an expected 'sabbath' of a thousand years when the Messiah would reign and the world's history would be fulfilled. Thus, the sabbath came to stand both for the perfection of the original creation and for its hoped-for renewal in a 'golden age', when all would be as God planned.

Luke's Gospel, placing the transfiguration after 'about eight days', introduces a significant variation, which no doubt reflects the Christian usage of celebrating the resurrection of Jesus on the day after the Jewish sabbath. The hoped-for renewal of the world is directly linked with the resurrection of Jesus, and transfiguration is a foreshadowing of that resurrection. For all three gospel-writers, however, 'transfiguration' is about far more than just some mysterious transformation in Jesus' appearance. Picking up the theme of the ages-long Jewish expectation of deliverance from oppression, they declare that this renewal of the world is to be brought about in consequence of the challenge to authority to which Jesus has set himself.

Second, Moses and Elijah. In the Old Testament, both are associated with significant events which take place – like the transfiguration – in mountain locations: Moses receives the tablets of the law, Elijah hears the voice of God. The 'holy mountain' is the appropriate place for special revelations. What was revealed to Moses at Mount Sinai was the way in which the righteous God – the God who had rescued his people from slavery in Egypt – both demands and, through the law, makes possible justice and freedom for his people. What was revealed to Elijah at Horeb (1 Kings 19:1-18) was that his resistance to the tyrant Ahab was not the lone struggle it had appeared to be; that there were 'seven thousand in Israel' willing to respond to the prophetic call to remain loyal to the God of justice and righteousness.

Moses and Elijah, representing law and prophets, are symbols of a tradition which is not just narrowly 'religious', but which is also social and political: a tradition concerned with justice for the poor, the alien, the orphan, the widow. In the same way, 'transfiguration' is not just a private religious experience vouchsafed to Jesus and the members of his inner circle;

it concerns 'the destiny he is to fulfil in Jerusalem' (Lk 9:31) – a destiny involving challenge to the established powers and authorities, in order that a new world may come into being: a world modelled upon that pattern of justice which is the righteousness of God himself.

But – third – while 'transfiguration' is about politics, it is also, in the words of Lehmann's title, about the *transfiguration* of politics. It is not just about confirming 'business as usual' for the powers that be. Rather, it is about an in-breaking of something new; it is about perceiving a new vision, receiving a new inspiration. It is about the understanding that the things of this world – including the world's politics – can be 'transfigured', given a new and greater significance. To quote Lehmann, 'In the brightness of that light, the world was being made all over again, and an invitation was being heralded abroad to join in a new celebration of the Sabbath when God looked upon everything that he had made and called it "Good!" and the whole human running race shouted in reply: "It is very good indeed!"'.[5] It is also – to remind ourselves again both of the context of the transfiguration story, and also of what we have ourselves said on previous pages – about the understanding that such a transformation is possible only if there are those who are prepared 'to suffer much ... to be put to death', albeit as a prelude to the 'being raised again' which equally is promised.

Something of this sort, we dare to suggest, was experienced in the women's groups during the coal strike. Through all the struggling and all the pain, the birth of something new was being glimpsed (women, after all, have their own powerful experience of new-birth-through-pain): and it was seen that such a new birth could only take place through a challenge to the powers and authorities of this world. Through the women's groups, women came to realise that they are a force to be reckoned with; that together they have an inner strength, enabling them to achieve what previously they could never have dreamed of.

Among the powers and authorities they had to face, of course, there were their own menfolk and the miners' union. Many miners openly acknowledge that without the help of the women the strike could not have lasted so long; but there are nevertheless many who still view the women's involvement with ambivalence. The women have not only – in spite of all the struggling – enjoyed the strike, in the way in which people do enjoy pulling together against a common enemy, enduring hardships with others. They have also found the chance to spread their wings and achieve. They have experienced many new and unexpected things – addressing public meetings both in Britain and abroad, sharing the abuse and violence of the picket lines as well as the gratitude and warmth of the food kitchens. They have become a force to reckon with; no longer 'just housewives'. This is, not surprisingly, something which many men find it hard to accept. The strike has transformed the women who were involved in the groups: some would say Margaret Thatcher has done more for them than she would ever care to admit.

We do not think it is too much to suggest that the transformation in the women of the mining communities, the new visions which were seen, the new understandings which were created, amount to an experience which can be equated with the New Testament experience of 'transfiguration'. The women have not been defeated, they have been re-born; perhaps, even, resurrected. They are now much more aware of themselves and of what is happening, both in this country and abroad. They have discovered a new commitment to do what they can to help bring about a new future, not only for their own communities but for others, too. That is why they are committed to maintaining their new-found links – with the Greenham Common women, whose experience they now understand and in some measure have shared; with the trade unions like NUPE and the NUT, whose support they have greatly valued. Many are joining the Labour Party, becoming involved in the nuclear issue, or are committed more locally to working within their communities with both young and elderly people. Meanwhile, their most immediate task is to support the families of sacked miners and to support both men and women who have to appear in court as a result of arrests during the strike.

There are those, of course, who say that the women's groups are no more than a seven-day wonder, that nothing has fundamentally changed. It is indeed doubtful that they will continue in their present form, but equally is it unlikely that the women who were involved will be able to return to life just as it always was. They will continue to be involved, to influence what happens in and around Barnsley and much further afield too. Women Against Pit Closures is setting up a permanent national organisation, and is considering the establishment of educational programmes for miners' wives, particularly in trade union and political studies.

Transfiguration, however, is not the end of a process; it is just a stage on the way. The New Testament story is followed by a return down from the mountain, to a world which objectively is no different from the way it was before the ascent. There is still sickness to be healed. The confrontation in Jerusalem is still to come.

Yet not everything is the same. A new vision has been gained, a new commitment entered, a new determination established. Similarly, when one asks the women in the women's groups about the future, one reply is always given, in a way which some might find threatening, but which others will see as a sign both of determination and of promise:

'We're organised now'.

CHAPTER EIGHT

HARSH ECONOMICS

In 1934, an explosion and fire at Gresford Colliery, North Wales, claimed 265 lives.

For many, this was the final nail in the coffin of the private colliery owners. They had scant regard for health and safety; their pits were small and, for the most part, inefficient and crying out for new investment. By 1947, the coal industry was virtually in a state of collapse, and quite unable to fuel the post war industrial boom. That was the year when the 980 collieries and all the unworked coal in the United Kingdom were nationalised, in one of the most popular acts of the Attlee Government.

In the immediate post war years, demand for coal grew steadily and, by and large, the industry prospered. By the 1960s, however, coal consumption had begun to decline under the combined impact of the introduction of smokeless fuels, the low price of oil, and coal's poor market image. Inevitably, this meant pit closures.

In fact, between 1947 and 1970, a total of 663 pits closed, leaving a mere 317 in production, although these dramatic figures mask the fact that in the early years of the period, many very small pits closed as a result of rationalisation rather than a fall in demand.

These gloomy trends for coal, however, were suddenly thrown into reverse by the Yom Kippur War of 1973, and the quadrupling of oil prices that resulted. The NCB submitted a Plan for Coal in 1974, which would involve £600m of new investment, and an increase in output of 40 million tonnes, from 130 million in 1970 to 170 million tonnes in the year 2000. The NUM warmly welcomed the Plan, and the new Labour Government immediately began to put it into effect.

Five years later, a new Government, committed to the free play of market forces, was installed in Whitehall. The impact on coal was summarised by a Monopolies and Mergers Commission report:

'The new Government in 1979 adopted a more financially oriented approach, and instituted a tight External Financing Limit. The NCB told us that in 1980 in order to meet the constraints imposed by this limit, to deal with the financial problems caused by the effects of the recession on sales and to get output and demand into balance in the short term, whilst protecting the longer term investment in the industry, it had .... decided that it would be necessary to accelerate the rate of colliery closures during the following three years'. (1)

At first, in 1980 and 1981, the NUM successfully resisted closures, but in the financial year 1982/83 7 pits closed, and up to January 1984 a further 12 pits shut down, with a total loss of 26,000 jobs.

In Autumn 1983, Ian MacGregor was appointed to head the NCB. In his first interview he stated his determination to accelerate the rate of pit closures and introduce high technology into 'super pits', with the aim of 'converting resources .... into an economic product at a price customers are willing to pay'. (2)

Cortonwood, and the year-long mining strike, were not far away. Perhaps even more chilling for the coalfield communities was the statement by Peter Walker, Secretary of State for Energy, in Cambridge 1982, that nuclear power generators 'can play a significant role in helping to keep down the price of electricity in the U.K.'.

At that date, 69% of NCB output – 87 million tonnes – was consumed by the Central Electricity Generating Board. At the Sizewell 'B' Public Inquiry, the CEGB have made it quite clear that they wish to replace coal and oil-fired generators with nuclear power.

Government and Electricity Board appear to be at one in their intentions. Whatever the rights or wrongs of the nuclear option, there can be little doubt that its impact on mining communities would be disastrous.

In the same Cambridge speech, which was in effect a definition of current UK Energy Policy, the Secretary of State appears to assign coal to at best a lowly, supporting role. It is just one energy source among others, and cannot be protected, since this would distort the market. If foreign sellers can undercut the NCB, then so be it. There is no planning strategy for British Coal, or North Sea Gas or Oil. Their positions will depend simply on world market prices.

In 1971, over 30% of residents of the Metropolitan Borough of Barnsley in employment worked in mining. By 1981, the proportion had fallen to 22%, or 19,500 Barnsley residents.

Even now, few communities can be so dominated by a single industry. Although the town of Barnsley has seen new industrial and white collar jobs expand since the seventies, the villages on the eastern side of the Borough are classic mining communities where everything revolves around the local pit.

Eavesdrop on any conversation in a local pub or club and it will only be a matter of minutes before there is talk of the Union, or 'the Board', or a machine breakdown, or problems at the new face. Missing fingers, scars, old men with acute breathing problems, widowed housewives, all bear testimony to the tough and dangerous life of the miner.

A gravestone at Silkstone Parish Church, erected to the memory of twenty-six children between the ages of 8 and 17, not only recalls the kind of disaster that used to be all too frequent, but helps explain the distrust for those who would seek to return the mines to private hands. The inscription reads:

> 'On that eventful day, the Lord sent forth his thunder, lightning, hail, carrying devastation before them, and by a sudden eruption of water into the coal pits of R. C. Clark Esq., 26 human beings whose names are recorded here were suddenly summoned to appear before their Maker. Reader remember – every neglected call of God will appear against thee at the day of judgement. Let this solemn warning then sink deep into thy heart to so prepare thee that the Lord, when he cometh, may find thee watching.'

The great bulk of Barnsley miners work in 18 pits within or very near the borough boundary. These pits fall within the Barnsley, Doncaster and South Yorkshire Areas of the Coal Board. A merger of Barnsley and North Yorkshire, and Doncaster and South Yorkshire with each other, was announced on the 28th March 1985.

It is highly significant that of all the Board areas, only Barnsley and

North Yorkshire planned to increase output in 1984/85. Everywhere else, a decline was projected.

In 1974, a dramatic renewal of the Barnsley Area began under the Plan for Coal. For many years previously it had exhibited what its Director called 'the effects of years of under-investment, i.e. closing collieries, falling output, a diminishing workforce and a lowering of its morale'. But then, in 1976, the first instalment of over £400 million worth of new investment began the transformation of a network of 18 collieries, which by 1984 were to see their entire output concentrated at three main handling points, with massive new washeries and computerised transport and loading on to the 'merry-go-round' rail system, feeding power stations in the area around the clock.

In a few short years, the Barnsley Area had become one of the most modern and technically efficient deep mining organisations in the world. Only North Yorkshire's Selby Complex has received more investment from the Board. Inevitably, though, the investment did not stem the loss of jobs – in fact, the new technology on which it was based shook out labour almost as fast as if there had been pit closures. Between 1977 and 1983, the workforce fell by over 2,000 and 1,000 more 'technology' losses were projected by 1986.

The prospects for jobs in the other two Areas where Barnsley miners work were, however, far worse. No significant investment was made or is planned. Between 1977 and 1983, 3,500 jobs were lost, and a further serious decline now seems inevitable in the aftermath of the strike. Three of the four pits in the South Yorkshire Area (Cortonwood, Wath and Manvers) are now closed or on the verge of closure, and in the Doncaster Area, the Highgate colliery has already closed, while Hickleton, a heavy loss maker, is to be shut down temporarily for 're-development', although most local people suspect it will never re-open. Only Goldthorpe appears to have a future. On the MacGregor principles, then, 5 out of 7 pits in the wholly mining villages on the south east rim of the Barnsley borough appear to be doomed.

It is not only the number of jobs that are changing; it is their quality also.

Mechanisation of mining operations proceeded apace during the 1960s and '70s. The installation, maintenance and repair of the coal shearers and other machines demanded a highly skilled workforce. Mining, mechanical and electrical skills were at a premium. In the three years to 1981, over 150 mining apprentices per year were passing through Barnsley College of Technology. But the Board's plans changed, and it informed the Business and Technical Education Council that from 1984 through to at least 1987, it would be placing no more mechanical and electrical engineering apprentices in colleges around the country.

This change befell the industry chiefly as a result of MINOS (Mine Operating System), a computerised system which enables operators in control rooms at the surface immediately to locate and diagnose faults in the machinery below ground. Whereas previously a breakdown would have meant skilled men spending up to several hours searching for the fault and then repairing it, now it could be done in seconds, and the faulty component replaced immediately with a new one, thus reducing 'down time' to an absolute minimum and enabling the process of extracting, transporting and preparing of coal to be carried out on assembly line principles.

The impact of MINOS on productivity can be dramatic. An NCB model of a colliery with 3 faces shows that, without MINOS, there is a need for 114 men per shift; with an advanced MINOS system, only 60 men are required, for the same output, a saving of 54 men. The total effect of MINOS has been both to de-skill the task and to reduce the number of miners.

The National Union of Mineworkers nevertheless favours new technology investment 'on a wide scale in all coalfields both to improve working conditions and reduce working time'.

Throughout the mining strike, the public was invited to believe that, however much sympathy there might be for mining communities, it was naive to imagine that coal could continue to be mined from hopelessly 'uneconomic' pits. Once this label was stuck on a colliery, there was little more to be said. But what if the demand for coal was to grow either suddenly or gradually? What if the Coal Board were to open up big new markets? What if a future Government decided to abandon the nuclear option? What will happen when North Sea oil and gas run out? What if the current world glut of oil becomes a shortage?

If any one of these easily conceivable developments occurs, the demand for coal would rise and an 'uneconomic' pit could become economic. There would be little point saying, 'it's a pity we shut that pit 5 years ago; we could do with it now.' Once closed, it is rarely possible to re-open a mine, and then only at inordinate cost.

As E. F. Schumacher, the author of *Small Is Beautiful* and one time adviser to the NUM, put it: '.... we must recognise that the concepts of "economic" and "uneconomic" cannot be applied to the extraction of non-renewable resources without very great caution... To eliminate the losing factory means the elimination of waste. But to close the losing colliery means merely to change the time sequence in which finite resources are being used.' (3) The crux of coal's present crisis is that demand for energy is well below expectation, so that new capacity is coming on stream which was originally intended to replace exhausted capacity. Now, instead, it amounts to spare capacity.

If the 1974 plan to use 170m. tonnes annually by the year 2000 had been sustained, there would have been little talk of uneconomic production. Under the new dispensation, there is no indication of what output targets ahead are to be, although it can confidently be stated that whatever they are must be well below the 1974 planned level.

What is quite clear is that a total of 25m. tonnes of new production is coming on stream now, fed equally by the Selby complex and by existing collieries being re-organised and equipped with new technology. Of this, only 9m. tonnes is needed to replace exhausted seams. This leaves 16m. tonnes to be eliminated from high cost pits.

Underlying this simple arithmetic is the fact that Selby's coal will need only 3,500 workers, whereas, to produce only slightly more now, Scotland and South Wales together need 39,000 men.

Perhaps the most chilling statistics of all are those with which Mr. Jonathan Winterton of Bradford University concludes a study on the combined impact of technology and the opening of new and the closure of old capacity. He predicts that by 1990, up to 80 collieries and 108,000 jobs will be lost.

Barnsley will suffer. It has both super-pits where technology is cutting jobs, and high cost pits which will close.

On 16th May the Board announced that 3,000 jobs were to be lost in

Barnsley through the closure of Emley Moor and Darfield Main. Emley's demise had been expected, because its seams were thin and all but exhausted. The announcement that Darfield was to close was, however, a bombshell.

Expert predictions had assumed that recent investment would keep it operating into the next century. In the end, Darfield was reprieved, but several other Barnsley pits, thought to be secure, are to close or are under threat from the most recently-announced production figures.

These are the opening shots of a threatened bombardment of the Barnsley coalfield, which neither NCB Enterprises, nor any other job-creating agency, has a hope of combatting.

CHAPTER NINE

LOOKING FORWARD

Towards the end of November 1985, a small group of people representing the Division of Social Responsibility of the Methodist Church met with the Secretary for Energy, Mr Peter Walker, and some of his senior civil servants responsible for the coal industry. The group included two of the contributors to this book. After the meeting, a letter was sent to Mr Walker offering the group's reflections. The letter included comments like these:

> 'We are deeply concerned about the social consequences of current economic and industrial policies. Members of the delegation have first-hand knowledge of the distress, demoralisation and disintegration that is now affecting the areas from which they come, and wished to share this with you and your officers during the course of the meeting.
>
> '... You and your officers told us several times that the government "cares". The reality is that many people in our country do not perceive the government to be a caring government and we know that, in the mining areas of which delegation-members have knowledge, it is not experienced as being so. This results not from a failure in presentation of policy, but from an experience of the impact of policy.
>
> 'We, and countless others within the nation, remain to be convinced that HM Government is sufficiently aware of and responsive to the social costs of its economic and industrial policies and to the disproportionate burden of costs being borne by particular groups in our society. We believe that HM Government is under a moral obligation to ameliorate the social effects of its policies, to ensure that the costs (and benefits) of economic transition are shared equitably'.

More positively, the letter also welcomed the establishment of NCB (Enterprises) Ltd 'as a significant and important initiative' in the creation of 'new employment opportunities in areas affected by pit closures', although it also questioned whether this could be a sufficient response. In general, and to no-one's great surprise, the impression gained by the group was that there was little likelihood of any significant change in existing government policies toward the areas of the country affected by pit closures.

Yet we do not believe that this book has to end on a negative note. We believe that there are grounds for hope for the future of South Yorkshire's mining communities. We believe this partly because, as Christians, we are convinced that there is always at work in human affairs a Spirit of God, who constantly inspires the creation of life which is full and whole. We believe it also because, during the strike, we have seen the emergence of many skills and talents. We have seen much self-discovery, much growth in new self-awareness, and we believe that the resourcefulness which the strike revealed could well become the basis for a new, different, yet very exciting future for our communities.

A major consequence of pit closures, and of the high level of unemployment which results, is poverty. Not only are individuals and families poor, but there is also a more general poverty which comes to affect the whole community as the circulation of money falls in the local economy – in shops, pubs, clubs and so on.

But when we say 'poor', we have to ask 'poor by what standards?' At this point, some Christian thinking is necessary. As we have already glimpsed in some of our earlier chapters, over against the real or impending 'poverty' of the mining communities – as measured by the standards of the consumer society, of the advertisers, of the years of full employment – there remain also immense resources of skill and talent in individuals. There is also a community network which even before the strike was stronger than in many parts of Britain, and which now because of the strike has been yet further strengthened.

Even in the days of relative affluence, there were many unmet needs. Proper health care was not easily available to chronic sick or to very old people. Education passed many people by. Families with several children – especially single parent families – still had to struggle hard. Provision of good food and entertainment was, at best, partial – more common was the flood of convenience foods and the competition for audience between the television channels. At a time of high unemployment, to try to re-capture the life of the 1960s and '70s is a false aim. How much more, then, must we avoid trying to re-capture the false images of those decades.

Rather, let us begin by recognising that within our communities there exist, as there have always existed, both many unmet needs and also many under-used human resources. Some, although certainly not all, of these needs – some provision of food, some repair of property and equipment, some personal and social services – can be met from resources which already exist within the communities. During the time of full employment, many of the skills which might make this possible remained dormant within people, unstimulated or even suppressed.

In many ways, the connection between needs and resources has been poorly met by the commercial world. The 'big money economy' failed to meet many people's most fundamental needs. It took the community kitchens of the strike to make many people aware that they had skills not only in cooking, but also in financing, organising and delivering services to people on a considerable scale.

The future for many of the communities of South Yorkshire will almost certainly be one in which past failures of the 'big money economy' will be multiplied, and there is good reason to suppose that the same will be true in the foreseeable future for many other parts of Britain, too. Christians, who for a long time have been told that we cannot serve both God and money, ought not to be surprised by such developments. Rather should we ask what it means to serve God rather than money – in order to gain some new insight into some possible alternative future for communities where money is seriously lacking.

Certainly, any theology of work will founder if it simply equates 'work' with 'paid employment'. Instead, we should see 'work' as that which meets people's needs and expresses a natural, human and God-given creativity. Usually, too, it involves *group* activities. It is on the basis of perceptions such as these that we begin to see again how skill and need may be brought together in more creative ways than happens in the 'big money economy'.

The New Testament offers us a number of starting-points for a reconsideration of the meaning and significance of work in human life. A particularly interesting one is the story Jesus told (Mt 20:1-15) of the landowner who hired men to work in his vineyard. Some were taken on early in the morning, some later in the day, and some only an hour before sunset. Yet, at the end of the day, all received equal pay, no matter how many or how few hours they had worked.

It is interesting to contrast this story as it is found in the New Testament with a similar story, told at a later date by some of the Jewish rabbis. Their version is similar, but it has one crucial difference: the worker who worked for only a short time in this version received full pay *because he had done more work than anyone else.* He had fully earned his pay, and the purpose of the story was precisely to extol his excellence. In the story as told by Jesus, however, the latecomers do nothing to earn their equal pay. 'Surely', says the landowner, 'I am free to do what I like with my own money. Why be jealous because I am kind?'

In the contrast between the two versions of that story, we see the difference between two worlds: the world of merit, and the world of grace.

The story, interestingly, was told by Jesus at a time, like ours, of high unemployment. Relief works were instituted in Jerusalem to create work for 18,000 unemployed men – the Manpower Services Commission has indeed a long pre-history! Against that background, God is depicted as an employer who has compassion for the unemployed and their families; as one who is not concerned about people getting what they deserve or what they have earned, but rather that they have enough to live on. The story is about a large-hearted man, compassionate and full of sympathy. This, says Jesus, is how God deals with people, and so he appeals to men and women to deal with each other in the same way – 'Why be jealous because I am kind?' (1)

The story presents us with an image of a world which cuts across many of the attitudes, expectations and values of the world we actually live in. It points to a world where people count for more than money. It points to a God who is constantly working to make the world into a place where that is so. It points to the need for women and men who will work with him; who, like the landowner, will be prepared to behave in 'odd' ways, sometimes at great personal cost. It changes our perceptions of what is and what is not 'fair'.

Traditionally, the church has extolled the virtues of honest labour: the need to do 'a fair day's work for a fair day's pay', to see daily work not just as a means of keeping alive but as nothing less than an offering to God of the gifts and talents he has entrusted to us. Such an understanding, however, might be thought unrealistically romantic in the context of an industrial system like ours, where many workers, including even many with high levels of skill, are seen as instantly disposable; where work is controlled not by workers themselves but by decision-makers in remote offices and board-rooms; where all the theory and knowledge which was once the prized possession of skilled crafts-people has progressively been systematised into mechanical rules and procedures, and even into computer programs.

Another story which Jesus told is about a man who entrusted his capital to three of his servants (Mt 25:14-30), two of whom faithfully traded with their shares and doubled them, while the third, to his master's great displeasure, merely hid his share in the ground. This is usually interpreted as a story whose moral is that we should make full use of our talents, our skills and resources, rather than wasting them. At a time when large numbers of people, not only in Britain but all around the world, are unemployed, that is certainly not an irrelevant message. Yet if we penetrate the story more deeply, we find that it has another message, rather different, yet even more relevant to our condition because it is better able to come to terms with the real situation in which many people now find themselves in their daily life.

For this was a crisis-parable, directed at a deluded people, and even more at their leaders, in order to bring them to a realisation of their true situation. It's message: a catastrophe is coming. The rich man in the story, feared by his servants as an inconsiderate and greedy employer, rewards the two faithful servants with increased responsibility; but the emphasis is on the reckoning with the third servant. He tries to make excuses for his failure, but cannot do so, because he has behaved with inexcusable irresponsibility.

And the audience of Jesus – familiar from the Old Testament with the designation of leaders, rulers, prophets and priests as 'servants of God' – would have recognised in the irresponsible servant the leaders of their own nation. The day of reckoning was at hand, when God would reveal whether they had been faithful to their trust; when they would have to render account of how they had used the resources God had entrusted to them – whether they had used them in accordance with God's will, or whether, like the third servant, they had frustrated God's will by careless neglect. The time of judgment, says Jesus, will come as suddenly as the unexpected return of the rich man from his journey. Be prepared for the crisis! For the time is always critical for those who fail to make use of the skills and resources God provides for ordering our lives and our world. (2)

How critical, then, is the situation for an industrial and economic system, and for its political and commercial leaders, in which the real needs of women and men are not met; in which we are all turned into 'sources of labour power', to be bought and sold as the needs of an impersonal economic system may dictate; in which resources of skill built up through centuries are thrown on the scrap-heap. How critical it is when, day in, day out, year after year, the very essence of our humanity, our human talents to feel, to care, to love, to be happy, to build and create, to win battles, to achieve aims – all the things which make us truly human – have to be buried, while we earn wages in employment and spend them at the behest of the advertisers. A catastrophe is coming – unless we have the perception, the wisdom, the creativity to find a new way of living together.

What hope is there that this might happen?

Charles Handy, in a book called *The Future of Work*, suggests that, in addition to the formal big money economy (which we might call the 'white economy', although Handy himself does not use this term), there exist three other patterns of economic organisation in our society. (3) He labels them, respectively, the 'black', 'mauve' and 'grey' economies. We are all familiar with Handy's 'black economy', and there is certainly some of it in South Yorkshire. This is an economy of 'real' jobs, but which exists outside, or as far as possible outside, the net of taxation. 'Black economy' workers share with many other small scale businesses the belief that taxation and the legislative control of business, designed for the great corporations, is not appropriate for them.

Work in the 'mauve' economy is an addition to employment in the 'white' economy: the school teacher who also makes pottery and sells it from a small shop; the factory worker who has a printing press in the garage; the housewife who also caters for wedding receptions. It is seldom sufficient by itself to support workers and their families, but to call it 'pocket money work' would be to trivialise it. Many new businesses have begun this way, but Handy suggests that the special characteristic of 'mauve' work is that it begins with little capital. Instead, its main resource is the creativity and skill of the workers themselves.

The 'mauve' is often an extension of the 'grey', or household, economy. One of the great weaknesses of traditional economic definitions is that they exclude work we all do in cleaning, cooking, washing and repairing things within our own households and in our local communities, where no money changes hands in consequence of these activities. Yet in the experience of us all, and particularly in the experience of communities of high unemployment, this is work of a very significant kind. A feature of consumer societies is the amount of capital equipment many households have at their disposal for work of this sort. By conventional economic measures, much of this equipment is under-used. Transition to the 'mauve' economy often involves the commercial use of skills and equipment which hitherto have been made available to the household or to the community as gifts.

Against the background of Handy's suggestions, we may begin to speculate about what a Christian perception of work might mean for the mining communities, taking account of the New Testament images we have examined.

First: extending the 'grey economy'. One consequence of unemployment is that families and communities are forced back upon their own resources. Can those resources be shared, as they were during the strike, to make life more creative and to reduce the element of drudgery? Can we not cook for each other, clean each other's cars, repair each other's household equipment?

During the strike, one man came to a discussion meeting in a car which he thought, although he was not sure, belonged to his brother's neighbour; it seemed to be the common property of the people who lived in one small group of houses. Where families cannot afford the capital outlay expected in more affluent homes, is there some way in which cars, lawn-mowers, electric drills may be shared? In this way, perhaps, better and more powerful equipment might be obtained – and then we may be on the way to the 'mauve' economy. When a lawn-mower is used for no more than a few hours each week, why should we expect each household to have its own? This would not only involve a move from private to some level of communal use of equipment, it would also involve an attack on what has been called 'commodity fetishism': the way in which advertisers offer us not just goods, but goods with an aura, goods as symbols of their owners' status and success. The sharing of such goods may teach us a great deal about the greater value, not of goods themselves, but of the lives of people to whom we are linked by a common bond of mutual service. Thus may we begin to serve God in his people, rather than money symbolised by the goods it buys.

Second: building a new sense of community. Bruce Kenrick, in his book about the Protestant Parish in New York's East Harlem district, describes how one of the symptoms of the poverty of that community was the filthy state of the streets and other public places. Officially-designated play areas were often inaccessible because of the rubbish with which they were surrounded. When church workers involved a group of local volunteers in cleaning up the mess, they not only made these areas accessible to people; they also showed that there could be a new pride in the physical environment in which people lived. (3)

The towns and villages of South Yorkshire are often not the most attractive places, and many have derelict buildings and unused land which are both unused resources and also eyesores. There is room here for practical action to reclaim these resources for practical use or to improve the environment. This would not only help to meet people's needs, it would also strengthen pride and belief in the local community.

There are many community needs. Playgroups and nursery schools, for example, bring together the energies of many people. So do projects for older children, teenagers, unemployed young folk, and so on. Churches, even when they have few personnel who can be involved in such activities, often have premises which might be used. In all this, however, a barrier which has to be broken through is that between individual and family on the one hand and the community on the other. Instead of thinking of 'my' lawn-mower, 'my' children, 'my' church, can we begin to think of these things as 'ours' – as common possessions to be shared for the greater wellbeing of all?

Small developments of this sort, both at the physical and at the community levels, could be powerful signs of hope, encouraging people to begin again to believe that life can be good and purposeful.

Third: developing the 'mauve economy'. Here we move beyond voluntary action to activities involving money, activities established on a more formal legal and financial basis, although not into profit-oriented commercial activities which are in the sphere of the 'white economy'. The idea of the non-profitmaking community co-operative presents the kind of model we have in mind.

Thus, in a Hertfordshire village, Little Berkhamsted when the buses were withdrawn in the early 1970s a group of people clubbed together and, with the usual fund-raising activities, raised enough money to buy a 12-seater bus. Volunteer drivers were recruited, and the bus was used to run a no-fares bus service to the nearest town on three days a week, as well as for other local purposes. The bus was owned by the Berkhamsted Bus Society, set up for the purpose, which raised funds in various ways to run and maintain the bus. Recent developments – particularly the 1985 Transport Act – may have helped to make activities of this sort easier. At the same time, in an area of low car-ownership like South Yorkshire, where the cheap bus fares policy of the County Council is now under threat both from limits to local authority spending and also from the abolition of the Council, such activities in the future will be all the more necessary.

Another area for such developments might be that of equipment repair. As the repair of domestic equipment has become increasingly expensive, many people have developed their own DIY skills, and often acquired quite expensive equipment, too. The repair of motor cars is the most obvious instance, but washing machines, children's toys and many other types of equipment also are repaired in this way. The conscious sharing of skills and equipment through the formation of community co-operatives for equipment repairs would not only be a straightforward financial operation, it would also constitute an important move away from a 'throw-away' society toward the renewable society.

Mining communities, of course, are not alone in facing the decline of their industry, leaving little in its place. Throughout the North of England, and elsewhere, too, there are former industrial communities whose industries have declined in the same way. In the future, as capital-intensive 'high tech' industry needs fewer and fewer workers, the present crisis in South Yorkshire's mining communities could well become endemic. The mining communities, however, because of their history and their social structure, and perhaps, too, because of the experiences of the strike, could be well-placed to spearhead the discovery of new ways of working and living together. A larger proportion of local needs would be met from local resources. Moreover, through opening up access to those resources – to tools, to land, to skills – people could again become creatively productive.

Of course, processes such as we have outlined are not enough by themselves to provide all the basic goods and services which communities need. No community can live for ever simply by 'taking in each other's washing'. Even less can this sort of economic activity replace what has been provided by miners' wage packets – although it may make possible community life of a kind which the wage economy seemed to discourage. The people of

South Yorkshire's mining communities have a right to expect that, if they are being required to bear the brunt of Government policies for the re-structuring of the energy supply industry, they should receive some compensation for the pains they are having to bear.

Beyond that, indeed, they have a right to expect that an energy policy for the future will take account of a wider range of considerations than have informed recent policy-making. They have a right to expect that, before pits are closed, some account will be taken of the cost to the nation of ever-increasing levels of unemployment. More broadly, they have a right to expect that some room should be made for social considerations in economic planning. They have a right to expect that far greater credibility be given to the arguments for the extraction of all available coal from a pit before it is closed, since to extract coal while a mine is still operational is a far more realistic proposition than to re-open it at some indefinite date in the future. They have a right to expect that the talents and resources of their communities will continue to be used for the national well-being, and not simply squandered.

The people of South Yorkshire have as much right to jobs, to proper health and social services, to good education, to careful planning and a clean environment, as people in more prosperous regions. Simple justice demands no less, and we who have produced this book are committed to the fight for justice for the coal mining communities. At the same time, however, we believe that the present turmoils offer new possibilities for the future, and we are convinced that within our communities there exists a determination and a creativity which could make the possibilities real.

EPILOGUE

'Truly the Lord is in this place, and I did not know it' (Gen 28:16)

Those words from the Book of Genesis form part of the story of Jacob. It is an interesting story. Jacob has just left home in fear of his life. He has tricked his father into giving him the blessing which should have been his brother Esau's – and so, as the younger son, he has effectively cheated his elder brother of the inheritance which naturally would have been his. Now, because of the enmity his action has caused, he is forced to leave home.

It is a moment of great uncertainty. Where is he to go? What will the future bring?

'God give you dew from heaven
and the richness of the earth,
corn and new wine in plenty!
Peoples shall serve you,
nations bow down to you.
.....' (Gen 27:28-9)

Those had been the words of his father's blessing. But what chance was there that they were to be fulfilled?

And then, something happens. Jacob has a dream, in which he comes face to face with God himself. The blessing of his father receives it's confirmation in God's own words, and everything is changed.

Or is it? Jacob is still running away from his brother's anger. The future is still uncertain. The enmity at the heart of the family is still there. The promises of land, of descendants, of God's protection – they are still only words. Promises, but with no substance to them.

And yet, something is different. The blessing which Jacob received from his father has its confirmation from God. A miracle has taken place. The fleeing deceiver, the cheat, the trickster, has not only been accepted by God, but he has been given his place in God's purposes and his promises. Or, to put it another way, what has happened to Jacob is that his father's God has now become his God, too. Jacob has recognised that, in what seemed to be a God-forsaken desert, God is present. 'Truly the Lord is in this place, and I did not know it'. In Jacob, a new generation comes to know that God is to be trusted and to be obeyed.

What, then, of the mining communities, facing the future with a mixture of hope and fear – but mostly with far more fear than hope? Can they – and can their children and grandchildren – come to anything like Jacob's faith? Can they learn that there is a reality, underlying all the uncertainties, in which they can put their trust? Can they learn to say of South Yorkshire in the last decades of the twentieth century, 'Truly the Lord is in this place'?

In an 'Open Letter to the Prime Minister' published immediately after the end of the coal strike, the Editor of the *Sheffield Star* described the way in which the economy, the people and the spirit of South Yorkshire's mining communities had all suffered because of the strike, and called for government aid to help re-build the once-strong local communities. But he also expressed real determination on the part of the people to pick up the pieces and to rebuild what a devastating year had all but destroyed. 'Give us the tools', he wrote, 'and this area will get on with the job of rebuilding and retaking its rightful place once more as a powerhouse of the nation'.

Whatever the difficulties of doing so – and in the months since the end of the strike those difficulties have if anything increased – the strengths of South Yorkshire's mining communities remain enormous. The miners' own slogan claimed that 'The miners united will never be defeated'. In the event, the miners were not united. They were defeated, and that defeat has been followed by still greater signs of disunity, nationally if not within South Yorkshire. But the strengths revealed through the year-long struggle remain and, if they can be built upon, they may yet turn that defeat into the beginning of a new future.

Meanwhile, for the churches, opportunities for mission are all around. Supporting people in and through the stresses and strains which the future undoubtedly will bring, through pastoral care and counselling, through practical help and everyday good neighbourliness, through activities which meet the needs of children and of young people, are an important beginning.

But there is also an important task of prophecy to be performed. This includes encouraging debate, both locally and nationally, about such issues as energy policy, the nature of work and the future of work. It includes raising questions, like those we have raised in the previous chapter, about the appropriateness of a consumerist future, and showing the possibility of other ways of living together. It includes raising awareness of the wider economic and political processes which have led to the present plight of places like South Yorkshire. During the strike, many people did become very aware of many of these issues. They must not be allowed to forget them now.

Above all, the churches' main task will be a very traditional one, however new the forms in which it will have to be carried out. For one of the greatest needs will be for groups of people who will proclaim words of hope, and who will work to create signs of the reality of that hope, in what to many will look like a very hopeless future. It will be the task of enabling people to perceive, in what will often feel like a God-forsaken desert, that 'Truly the Lord is in this place'.

The 'agenda for mission' in the mining communities for the next decade and more will be enormous. Nothing less than all the resources which Christian faith has at its disposal will be enough to make it possible. In the preceding pages we have tried to show something of the scope of those resources. We do not doubt that they are sufficient, although we are well aware that we, like many of our fellow Christians, too often fail to draw sufficiently upon them. We pray not only for faith and hope to see what may be, but also for determination of will to make it possible.

In our struggle to find faith, hope and determination, we are at one with all the people among whom we live. With them, we struggle to believe that the future really does hold a promise; that it is worthwhile living for it; that there is a goal toward which we can journey in faith as did God's people of old and as will countless generations yet to come.

God says to Jacob, 'I will not leave you until I have done all that I have promised' (Gen 28:15).

'And be assured', says Jesus, 'I am with you always, to the end of time' (Matt 28:20).

APPENDIX:

Pastoral Care in Mining Communities – a check-list of possible actions

The following 'check-list' was issued by the Barnsley Methodist Circuit Meeting in March 1985.

> Various ministers, individual members and congregations have been giving practical help to families involved in the mining dispute since it began. This check-list is not intended to imply that nothing has been done. Still less is it seen as a set of actions which all must undertake.
>
> Rather it is a collection of suggestions which may help to focus attention on what needs to be done and ways of doing it. It is of course entirely a matter for local circumstances what specific actions are taken up.
>
> 1. Make efforts to offer friendship and support to isolated miners and their families.
> 2. Give support to individual pastors who are attempting to play a part in resolving the practical and family problems that exist now and will continue even though the strike is over.
> 3. Provide pastoral visiting and practical help for miners and their families as an integral part of the church's work.
> 4. Provide counselling, where appropriate skills are available, for individuals and families undergoing stress.
> 5. Provide welfare rights and debt counselling advice where skills exist or can be acquired.
> 6. Organise activities which recognise the particular needs of children and young people.
> 7. Make premises available for social and/or workshop activities.
>
> *8. Explore sources of finance to assist 7.
>
> *9. Explore industrial chaplaincy opportunities.
>
> 10. Urge those in a position to do so to create alternative jobs, and to improve the 'image' of the area, by environmental and social measures.

11. Consider organising a conference or retreat for those who need to share their problems and cope with stress.
12. Consider 'church twinning' with congregations in non-mining areas to secure wider understanding of our problems and enlist support.
13. Work to secure better understanding and improved relationships among all involved in the mining industry.
14. Become more involved in union and political processes.
15. Provide an industrial facet to such services as Harvest Festivals.
16. Place concerns about the future of our communities, and the way our problems can be met on Church Council/Committee agendas.
17. Encourage debate about issues such as the future of work, alternative forms of work and the use of leisure.
18. Be willing to talk, in a spirit of openness and tolerance, of the problems that face us.

* It is likely that these proposals would be best pursued at Circuit Level.

NOTES AND REFERENCES

Chapter Three

1. Robert Moore, *Pit-men, Preachers and Politics* (Cambridge University Press, 1974), pp 26f.

Chapter Four

1. See Bob Fryer, 'Trade Unionism in Crisis', in Huw Beynon (ed), *Digging Deeper: Issues in the Miners' Strike* (Verso, 1985), pp 74-7.

Chapter Five

1. Michael Crick, *Scargill and the Miners* (Penguin Books, 1985), p 109.
2. Sheffield Policewatch, *Taking Liberties* (1984).
3. National Council for Civil Liberties, *Civil Liberties and the Miners' Dispute* (1984), p 13.
4. As ref 3; p 11.
5. On the interpretation of Romans 13, see E. Käsemann, 'Principles of the Interpretation of Romans 13', in *New Testament Questions of Today* (SCM Press, 1969), especially pp 211f.
6. Gerd Theissen, *The Social Setting of Pauline Christianity* (T & T Clark, 1982).

Chapter Six

1. Jürgen Moltmann, *The Church in the Power of the Spirit* (SCM Press, 1977), p 166.

Chapter Seven

1. *Women Against Pit Closures* (Barnsley Women Against Pit Closures, 1984), p 6.
2. Loretta Loach, 'We'll be Here Right to the End ... And After: Women in the Miners' Strike', in Beynon (ed) (as ref to Chapter Four), p 169.
3. As ref 1; p 22.
4. Paul Lehmann, *The Transfiguration of Politics* (SCM Press, 1975). The following paragraphs do not directly present Lehmann's ideas, although they are considerably dependent upon his work.
5. Lehmann (as ref 4), p 93.

Chapter Eight

1. Monopolies and Mergers Commission Report, NCB, Vol 1 (June 1983), pp 72-3.
2. Ian MacGregor, 'My Aims for Coal', in *Coal News,* September 1983.
3. E. F. Schumacher, 'Coal – the Next 50 Years', in Britain's Coal (NUM Study Conference, March 25-26, 1960).

Chapter Nine

1. For the interpretation of this parable, see J. Jeremias, *The Parables of Jesus* (SCM Press, 1963), pp 136-139.
2. As ref 1; pp 58-62.
3. Bruce Kenrick, *Come Out the Wilderness* (Collins, 1962), p 55.

FOR FURTHER READING

Books about the strike and issues arising from it

Huw Beynon (ed)
Digging Deeper: Issues in the Miners' Strike (Verso, 1985)

Michael Crick
Scargill and the Miners (Penguin Books, 1985)

National Council for Civil Liberties
Civil Liberties and the Miners' Dispute (NCCL, 1984)

Welsh Campaign for Civil and Political Liberties
Striking back (WCCPL & NUM S.Wales Area, 1984)

Books about Christianity, Politics and Society

Rex Ambler & David Haslam (eds)
Agenda for Prophets: Towards a Political Theology for Britain (The Bowerdean Press, 1980)

Brian Jenner (ed)
Insights for Christian Opposition (COSPEC & Urban Theology Unit, 1984)

David Sheppard
Bias to the Poor (Hodder & Stoughton, 1983)

General Synod Board for Social Responsibility
Policing in a Democratic Society (Available from General Synod Board for Social Responsibility, Church House, Dean's Yard, London SW1)

How are we to achieve the major changes in perspective and orientation which will enable us today to participate in, and be useful to, the liberation and empowerment of the common people and their servants, the Christians?

It is a mammoth task. Part of the problem is that the institutions and learning processes of our society are geared to preserving and enhancing the very vested interests which perpetuate oppression. Education, the churches, community work, social work, even voluntary work and vocational work, all play their part in maintaining the *status quo.*

So, how can education, churches, community, social voluntary and vocational enterprises be taken over, here and there, by servants of the poor and pioneers of commitment and liberation?

Urban Theology Unit has for ten years built itself up "from the bottom", to try to serve this need. It is based on a sharing-caring community, almost wholly unpaid, of men and women who live in two or three pleasant but undeniably inner-city streets of north-east Sheffield.

UTU runs a Resource Centre, a Contemporary Library and the Dale Biblical Library, a Bookstore, a Community-Work Resource Room, and Houses for members and long and short-term visitors and students.

People come for a weekend, a week, a few weeks, a term, or for one or two years. They work at their own agendas, and use seminars, lectures and group work to develop their own ideas and get new ones. Subjects include Cities and People, Bible Study, Liberation Theology, Community Alternatives, Practical Visions. These involve 3-week Seminars.

Three times a year, groups come for our short courses – Come Down Our Street, Lord, and Vocation in the Eighties. Frequently, special groups meet with special agendas in our areas of concern.

UTU is a Charitable Trust, and is a Membership Association kept going by the commitment and generosity of 350 individuals. Members pay £10 or more yearly (unwaged £6) and get news of our work, copies of our publications, and involvement as they can in our work.

URBAN THEOLOGY UNIT
210, ABBEYFIELD ROAD, SHEFFIELD, S4 7AZ

NEW CITY JOURNALS

DOING THEOLOGY IN THE CITY – Vol. 2
New City 18 £1.00
Basic Texts on Urban Liberation Theology and Urban Training.
The Witness and Work of UTU, 1978-85.

INSIGHTS FOR CHRISTIAN OPPOSITION
New City 17 £1.00
Christian Organisations for Social, Political and Economic Change – Joint publication.

GOSPEL FROM THE POOR
New City 16 50p
Good News – from Poor Jesus, Poor People and Poor Churches. By Norwyn Denny, Margaret Mackley, David Moore and John Vincent.

WHAT CHURCHES CAN DO
New City 15 50p
Garth Rogers introduces Fifty Examples of Christians involved in Mission Alongside the Poor in Britain today.

TWO NATIONS – ONE GOSPEL?
New City 14 50p
Divided Britain, and how it affects Old People, Kids, Teenagers, Work and the Unemployed.